Praise for *Embrace the Middle*

Dr. Kaufmann writes beautifully, with a lovely, insightful, supportive, helpful, and warm tone. And about an under-discussed, important, and widely relevant topic. This is a useful, wonderful book!

Rick Hanson, PhD,
author of *Hardwiring Happiness* and *Buddha's Brain*

Embrace the Middle *offers a research-based, practical guide for women who are ready to be whole—to integrate presence, compassion, and embodied wisdom. Dr. Kaufmann guides us to ease into the many moving parts of midlife without the struggle. Sparkles of insight, even genius, mark the integration of our many parts with the wisdom of age.*

Margaret Moore, MBA, Founder and CEO,
Wellcoaches Corporation; Co-Founder/Chair Institute of Coaching

A book that every woman will want to share with her sisters and friends— and that every loving man who wants to understand his wife as she gets older must read.

Ken Druck, PhD,
author of *Courageous Aging* and *How We Go On*

Embrace the Middle *is more than a book—it is a movement rejecting the negative narratives so many women internalize about aging. Blending her expertise in deep meditation practice with insights informed by original research on over 600 women worldwide, Kaufmann encourages embracing the inevitable evolutions of midlife with grace and authenticity while unlocking your wisdom, power, and potential to truly blossom.*

Diana Chapman, Co-Founder,
The Conscious Leadership Group

Embrace the Middle *is a beautifully written inspirational guide to the varied experiences of midlife. Dr. Kaufmann shares her expertise and provides reassurance and helpful tools for traversing the terrain of the middle years. Readers will identify with and learn from the many stories she tells based on her own valuable experiences and those of the women she interviewed.*

Margie E. Lachman, PhD,
Fierman Professor of Psychology and
Director of the Lifespan Lab, Brandeis University

In her brilliantly written book, Embrace the Middle, *Shayna Kaufmann shares with us a comprehensive look at the challenges and joys of women's mid-years and provides us with a gentle and mindful system to deepen our experiences. Shayna's rich professional and spiritual background shines through in these pages as she encourages readers to be present to life's moments with love and compassion. As she shares her own challenges along with the those of other women, the reader gains a unique insight into one's own current attitudes toward these transformative years and is provided with practical ways to embrace them with acceptance, confidence, and joy. This book is a must read for any woman on the path of self-discovery!*

Michele Hébert, Raja Yoga Guide,
author of *The Tenth Door: A Yoga Adventure*

In my four decades of therapy practice, I've supported countless women navigating the complexities of midlife. Embrace The Middle *is a book I dearly wish I had to offer them during those years. It beautifully amalgamates cutting-edge developmental science, accessible spirituality, and poignant narratives of real women's experiences. Kaufmann seamlessly interlaces her own midlife journey with those of others, crafting a tapestry of relatable stories that capture the essence of the heroine's quest. From* career peaks to empty nests, from bodily changes to the deep yearning for self-love, the book explores the myriad challenges and joys of this pivotal stage.

Norma Burton, CEO,
Journey to Completion Healing Center,
author of *Lucid Dreaming, Lucid Living*

At long last the stigma of midlife stands a chance to be removed for generations to come. Dr. Shayna Kaufmann's Embrace the Middle addresses this stage of life with the dignity, honor, and curiosity that it deserves. Her use of humor, original research, authenticity, and her own raw vulnerability not only engage the reader from the start, but place her in your heart as a trusted source and friend. Her SOFTT method is a practical and accessible tool to use anytime and anywhere. Thank you, Shayna, for revealing this stage of life for all that it is and has the potential to be.

Kate Byrne, Co-Founder,
The Tulle Box, and Good Light Capital

Dr. Kaufmann does a masterful job capturing the essence of "The Middle" and uses her expertise, intuitive insights, and research to demonstrate how to embrace this vital phase of life. Her SOFTT tool gives you step-by-step guidance to disengage from your thoughts, in the moment, improving and expanding your perspective and outcomes. I will keep a copy of this book with me as a constant reminder of what is possible.

Kelley Kurtzman, Former CSO,
Verizon Executive

Embrace the Middle *is a wonderful reminder of the ways women benefit from allowing life to change them rather than trying to cling to their youth. Dr. Kaufmann listens carefully to the experiences of women and encourages them to authentically give voice to the gifts they have to share as they live in the middle chapter of their life. She mixes tools from various resources and offers her own SOFTT practice in a manner that helps us cope with everyday life challenges. She creates a clear pathway for women to recognize their offering and return to confidence in themselves as they move forward in the years ahead.*

Diane Moore, Teacher,
Santa Rosa Zen Group

Embrace the Middle *offers the same transformative impact Dr. Kaufmann demonstrates in her teachings and workshops. Her profound personal insights and practical techniques are accessible to all. I highly recommend* Embrace the Middle *for anyone seeking to explore a compassionate and illuminating approach to life's changes, joys, and challenges.*

Jodie Grenier, CEO,
Foundation for Women Warriors

EMBRACE
—THE—
MIDDLE

A Woman's Guide to Mindfully Navigating the Challenges, Celebrating the Joys, and Finding Power in Midlife

Shayna Gothard Kaufmann, PhD

EMBRACE THE MIDDLE

A Woman's Guide to Mindfully Navigating the Challenges, Celebrating the Joys, and Finding Power in Midlife

By Shayna Gothard Kaufmann

1. BODY, MIND & SPIRIT / Mindfulness & Meditation
2. SELF-HELP / Aging
3. SEL016000 SELF-HELP / Personal Growth / Happiness

ISBN: 979-8-88636-044-8 (paperback)
ISBN: 979-8-88636-045-5 (ebook)

Cover design by Lewis Agrell

Printed in the United States of America

Authority Publishing
13389 Folsom Blvd #300-256
Folsom, CA 95630
800-877-1097
www.AuthorityPublishing.com

DEDICATION

To Eric, Tara, and Maya,

Words cannot convey my depth of love and
gratitude for the three of you.
You are my greatest source of inspiration, pride, and joy.

To Mom, Dad, and Eddie,

My profound sorrow over your passings is commensurate
with my love for you each.
Your departures taught me how to fully grieve,
fully live, and fully love.

CONTENTS

Appendices

INTRODUCTION

It was a beautiful summer evening in 2015. The soft dusk light was accentuated by a gentle breeze and the magical sounds of a nearby string quartet. The scene took place at a gala, where I was happily sipping a delicious, chilled Prosecco while chatting with two women whom I had just met. We smiled widely at one another, as a waiter refilled our wine glasses, and eagerly accepted another round of stuffed mushrooms. It was a perfect evening.

That is, it *was* perfect until one of the women turned to me and asked the customary, "So what do you do?" My mood instantly plummeted, I felt a familiar discomfort spring up in my stomach, and I am certain that my happy smile disappeared.

After hesitating, I flatly replied, "I'm a forensic psychologist. I evaluate criminal defendants." Their reactions were expected and familiar. "Wow!" said one and "Tell me more!" replied the other as she scanned the area looking for a waiter to top off our wine glasses. Both women even moved a few inches closer, as if eagerly awaiting my next words.

To be fair, I enjoyed this kind of interest in my twenties and thirties, when my work was intellectually stimulating and exciting. I liked debunking popular myths while answering people's curious questions. "Are you ever scared?" some asked. "Yes," I answered. "There have been a few times when I felt uneasy, and even scared, but nothing ever happened to me." "Is it hard being around murderers and rapists?" others asked. "Sometimes," I would reply, "especially the unrepentant sex offenders. But I get to know their entire story, and put that in context of their offenses." One even asked, "Are you like that woman on CSI?" "No," I'd say. "And I definitely don't look or dress like her. I intentionally wear modest and bland clothing to not attract any extra attention."

But alas, I had changed over the decades, and with my evolution, my relationship to my work had changed as well. I quickly learned that my clients, whom I had seen more as "subjects," were human beings with deeply sorrowful childhoods and life courses. Seldom were their situations cut-and-dry; their backstories contained significant factors that contributed to their behavior. And their poor choices had profound ripple effects. I was usually sad, and often disturbed, when I left my interviews with clients.

My work became more challenging in my late thirties, when I became a mother to my two beautiful daughters, Tara and Maya. I was in awe of them and of motherhood. My girls were surrounded by love and care and had lives of privileged opportunity ahead of them. The contrast was so very stark between my daughters' fortunate upbringing and my clients' common histories of trauma, familial drug addiction, and limited resources. Motherhood was fun, bright, and hopeful. My work was difficult, dark, and depressing.

My meditation practice, which I started when my daughters were one and three, added another layer of deep contrast to my professional world. Meditation opened up an unexpected Pandora's box of tools and personal insights. I was introduced to practices like lovingkindness, staying with discomfort, and observing my crazy "monkey mind." Meditation was an exciting, fresh, and hopeful approach to life, and it offered a path to my lifelong soul-searching. I started meditating with increasing regularity, meeting with my teachers weekly, and attending several meditation retreats per year.

I had no idea how powerful the seemingly simple act of sitting still could be, nor that it would become a cornerstone of both my life and future work.

The distaste for the darkness of my forensic work grew in direct proportion to my love of motherhood and meditation. By my mid-forties, that distaste turned to dread. Going to jails began to feel like my own form of incarceration. I recall driving to work, fantasizing what it would feel like if this were my last case (definitely not a good thought to have on the way to work). I felt weighed down as I walked the dank, isolated corridors, through the gray metal doors that loudly locked behind me. I was relieved when my interviews were over. Oddly, I also felt a sense of guilt as my clients watched me exit through doors that unlocked for me, while they remained handcuffed to a table.

That jolt of discomfort I experienced when talking with those women at the gala was due to me feeling wildly inauthentic with regards to my profession. My chosen work was not just stale; it had begun to suck the life force out of me. I was being disingenuous to myself and my clients, by staying in a career I had long outgrown. With my fiftieth birthday looming, it was imperative that I make a change soon. Otherwise, it would be a lifelong regret.

I had an "aha" moment during a meditation retreat a few months after that gala, which sparked my next professional endeavor. The inspiration was, of all things, a menopausal hot flash. I discovered in real time that when I was mindfully present to my hot flash, it was far more helpful than my usual response of cursing and dramatically fanning myself. This "present hot flash experience" led to the epiphany that accepting, rather than rejecting, inevitable midlife changes could potentially bring more ease, or even joy, into those decades.

And I was not just thinking about menopause. I was envisioning my aging parents, my daughters in their waning years of high school, and my literal expanding middle. In that moment, on the meditation cushion, I imagined starting a company dedicated to helping women more gracefully navigate midlife transitions. I would call it *Embrace the Middle*.

Little did I know that the multitude of midlife events I anticipated happening "down the road" would much sooner become my heartbreaking reality. In 2018, my mother, Jackie, died suddenly and unexpectedly from heart disease. In 2020, my father, Sol, succumbed to a courageous two-month battle with cancer. A mere seven months later, while I was still reeling from my father's death, my brother, Eddie, who was one of my best friends, and with whom I had just ushered out my father, also died suddenly and unexpectedly. Within the same window of losing my parents and brother, I made the difficult choice to discontinue practicing meditation with my long-term Zen teacher. That was a different kind of loss, yet still profound. I was overcome with grief.

I felt like one of those stand-up inflatable figures that gets knocked down, slowly wobbles back upright, only to get knocked down, again and again and again. There were many days when the tears would not relent and many nights when I had panic attacks as I lay in bed, fearful of receiving another dreaded, middle-of-the-night phone call.

This profound assault of midlife trials challenged me to walk the talk of gentle presence. I did my best to accept and stay present to my feelings and to life, rather than bury my sorrow or disappear into a cloud of detached grief.

Loved ones' deaths were just one part of those pivotal years. In the midst of those losses, I helped both of my daughters launch from the nest. One headed to Europe for a gap year and two years later, my youngest left for university in Northern California. I was thrilled with their growth, but being an empty nester left my well-honed Mom identity suddenly and significantly whittled down. This was not a bad milestone. In fact, my husband and I adapted relatively quickly and love our quieter space. But it was still another profound midlife transition.

Paradoxically, some remarkable, though more subtle, changes happened in that same time frame. As I went through (not got through) each compounding storm, I became acutely aware of my strength and resilience, and emerged stronger than I could ever imagine. I knew what I needed to do to take care of myself, and I was able to access my internal and external tools. My sense of personal agency, in the absence of four of the most influential people in my life, grew exponentially. Though I miss my loved ones terribly, I was fully capable of navigating life without their input or reassurance. Similarly, my spiritual growth was no longer dependent on a teacher; my decades of practice lives within me. Whether it was a result of my losses, or in addition to them, I came to know and embrace my power like never before.

Being confronted with so many losses, and especially unexpected and premature ones, also brought me face-to-face with my own mortality. I understood, on a visceral level, one of my Zen teacher's favorite sayings: "We are always skating on thin ice." And with that, I made many positive changes in my life. I phased out overly complicated friendships, choosing to enjoy more time with the treasured, deeper ones. I curtailed choices based on guilt and "shoulds," opening more deeply to what I authentically did and did not want. I looked for affiliations that were aligned with my heart rather than my history. I had already transitioned out of my forensic career, and re-embarked on my Embrace the Middle endeavor with renewed fervor and certainty.

I attribute my ability to navigate the seemingly unnavigable, the emergence of my power, and my positive life changes to two primary practices: presence and compassion. My husband was my rock, and my community my extended support, but presence and compassion were my internal anchors and external approach to healing and growth. It was only after these anchors were firmly rooted inside that I could truly benefit from the external layers of support.

Meditation, my formal practice of presence, provided the space for me to softly feel my myriad emotions and changing circumstances without running from them or getting lost in my thoughts. It was in those many hours of stillness "on the cushion" that I felt both the depths of my sorrow and my emerging strength, resilience, and solidity. I also practiced presence when praying, observing rituals around grief and transitions, and spending time in nature. These "off the cushion" activities were equally transformative.

Self-compassion was also paramount to my healing. I needed tenderness, not self-imposed pressure, time lines, or expectations. As a reminder to be gentle with myself, I regularly ended my meditation practice with a lovingkindness verse, for myself and for my family members who were also grieving. Self-compassion did not change my circumstances but it absolutely changed how I experienced them.

This book, however, is more than a reflection of my personal journey. It also includes the experiences of 619 women who completed my midlife survey in the latter part of 2020, and especially the subset of 103 women who volunteered to be interviewed to discuss their survey responses in intimate detail.

I will share a wealth of information about the female midlife experience, via anecdotes from many of the interviewees and quantitative data findings from the survey. These personal stories and survey data highlight our common midlife struggles and gifts, and the wisdom we have earned and learned along the way. I hope to illuminate and validate the multifaceted tapestry of this season.

I will propose an "embracing" approach to navigate the challenges and celebrate the gifts of midlife. For some readers, this approach may oppose conditioned ways of responding, such as the instinct to push away difficult experiences. Though avoidance of challenges can seem easier, it is seldom healing.

I will dispute the prevailing, overarchingly negative midlife paradigm and encourage women to become more aware of, and embrace, our earned growth and wisdom with the hope of illuminating a more empowered, fulfilling, and graceful path forward.

The book is organized as follows:

Part 1, What is Embracing and What is the Middle? In these chapters, I explain the three components of "embracing"—presence, compassion, and wisdom—and why I believe it can transform the midlife experience. Part 1 also includes a chapter on my research methods and questions, and explores the many ways to define "the middle." Lastly, I introduce SOFTT, my five-step process of *how* to embrace.

Part 2, What to Embrace. This section is drawn extensively from the survey and interview data. Two of the chapters present my quantitative and qualitative research findings regarding the challenges and gifts of midlife. The other two chapters detail how to apply the SOFTT approach in these varied contexts.

Part 3, Changing the Midlife Paradigm. Part 3 addresses the power of mindful awareness of the many co-occurring "ands" of midlife—the challenges and gifts, the losses and gains, the endings and beginnings—and includes a guided meditation. Chapter 10 relays some of the deep and beautiful wisdom shared by the interviewees. This book concludes with an appeal to us all to collectively change the overarchingly negative midlife narrative, challenge diminishing stereotypes, and bring awareness and resistance to sexism and ageism.

Though the details of my journey, and the journeys of the women whose stories I share, may be unique, the themes are universal. I want women to know that we are not alone, that we are not crazy, that we are not flawed, nor are we uniquely gifted in the increased awareness, clarity, and embodied wisdom that can accompany midlife. My hope is that readers will connect in validation and support, appreciate our similar and different journeys, and celebrate this powerful juncture in our individual and collective lives.

Part 1

What is Embracing
&
What is The Middle?

CHAPTER 1

THE ILLUMINATING HOT FLASH

"The only way to make sense out of change is to plunge into it, move with it, and join the dance."

— Alan Watts

It was a hot, muggy August afternoon (especially for San Diego), the kind of day that would have been perfect for an ocean swim. I was less than two miles from the beach, but doing nothing of the sort. Instead, I was sitting in a toasty, airless meditation hall, staring at a white wall, and sweating. We had just returned to meditating after our lunch break, on the third afternoon of a five-day meditation retreat. Sleepy, sticky, and fidgety, I was doing my best to be still and quiet when, out of nowhere, I felt the rising heat of an incoming hot flash. "Nooo!" I thought. "Go away! Seriously!? Shit."

I immediately forgot about meditating and began to mentally curse the hot flash, as if it were a demon overtaking my body. My mind flooded with a barrage of negative and self-pitying thoughts: "I can't believe this is happening now," "I'm already so f**king hot!" and ultimately, "This sucks." As these retreats entail a commitment to sit still, I imagined that I put my thick hair in a ponytail and frantically fanned myself with a folder stashed beneath my meditation cushion.

Clearly, none of this was helpful. In fact, I felt more miserable and powerless.

And then, almost as an afterthought, I remembered what I was supposed to be practicing: breathing, feeling my bodily sensations, and noticing my thoughts but without engaging with them. So, I ceased my inner kvetching, reconnected with my breath, and started to pay attention to my oodles of bodily sensations. I became aware of the pulsating heat around my head and neck, followed a trickle of sweat slowly rolling down my cheek, and felt a delightful coolness when an occasional breeze from the ceiling fan connected with my damp skin. I noticed that the hot flash sensations came on like an ocean wave; they rapidly crested, lasted for a moment, and subsided almost as quickly, leaving ripples of warmth in the aftermath.

I was so engrossed in the exploration of my hot flash that I jumped when the timekeeper struck the bell signaling the end of the thirty-minute meditation block. It was actually a very cool (pun intended) experience.

"Shit!" became "Shift." When I accepted rather than rejected the heat wave, and when I was present to the sensations instead of trying to make them go away, the entire experience transformed. Without the mental narrative, it was simply an intense, brief experience of heat. My impulse to push away the discomfort, my automatic complaining, and my desire to seek immediate relief (head in the freezer, anyone?) were reactive and partly driven by the dreadful lore I had internalized about hot flashes long before they ever began. This time, a hot flash was just that: a hot flash and nothing more. The negative inner narrative and reactive behaviors were optional, and added unnecessary suffering.

I was so thrilled by this epiphany that I decided to rename my menopausal hot flashes to "mental pauses." The onset of a hot flash became akin to a meditation bell, reminding me to pause, breathe, and mindfully pay attention to what was happening in my body. Rather than run from them, hot flashes became an invitation to be present. This was a vastly different, more welcoming way to relate to an unwanted experience.

And then came the "aha" moment—something that paradoxically can happen to many people who meditate for extended periods. What if I chose to be intentionally present to the many big midlife changes that were on the horizon—my parents' decline, my own physical changes and challenges, and my two daughters leaving for college? Rather than resist thoughts of these natural transitions, bury my feelings of fear and sorrow, and reject my aging, what if I were to simply accept their reality? My parents were declining and, unbeknownst to me at the time, both would very soon pass. Our daughters were close to graduating from high school and would be beginning their next chapters. And both my eyes and knees were seriously declining. To fight against these inevitable changes was physically and emotionally exhausting.

And my body image, those negative perceptions of my literal middle? I could not even calculate how much precious time I had wasted over the decades, and the self-induced misery I had caused, by rejecting my body, and myself by extension. "I hate my thighs," "I hate my stomach," and "I hate my hair," were automatic, ingrained thoughts, followed by (usually unsuccessful) efforts to change them. Love and acceptance were not even on my radar. I was overcome with remorse even considering it. I wanted to be kind to my body, grateful for all it had given me, and honor what it could still do, as well as what it could no longer do. In that sweaty moment on the cushion, "Embrace the Middle" was conceptually born. And it started with acceptance.

Accepting vs. Resisting

An overarching aspect of embracing is acceptance—accepting the reality of whatever is on our plates. Every stage of life poses difficulties, but midlife has some doozies: accepting our physical changes and decline, accepting our own and our loved ones' mortality, and accepting the potentially loud call for change (before it's too late).

Acceptance does not imply that we are at peace with any of these challenges. Indeed, most of us would rather dodge these difficult transitions. Nor does acceptance mean we should not use resources or get support to help with our struggles. Rather, acceptance affirms the inevitable realities of aging, which will happen regardless of our associated feelings. And, acceptance is a starting point to manage these changes with more grace.

When my mother started developing dementia, I did not want to believe this was her reality. She was a tireless leader, wife, mother, grandmother, and beacon of her community. I was pained even thinking about my mother being confused, uncertain, or dependent. But, as her symptoms increased over time, the truth became harder to refute.

Though it was difficult to accept the reality of my mother's condition, it was ultimately easier. Through research and support groups, I learned more about dementia, which helped me to better understand her behavior and respond with more sensitivity and compassion. I tried to imagine I was hearing each repetitive story for the first time, just as she believed she was telling it to me for the first time. And I could appreciate why my mother was more confused when I brought her somewhere less familiar, and why she was more at peace in her own home or yard.

To resist, or reject, is the opposite of accepting. It is the refusal to accept a situation. It is proclaiming, "No," "This can't be true," or "I don't want this." We resist when we keep our heads in the sand with busyness, numb our reality with alcohol, bury it with food, or use any other method to escape feeling our feelings. In my mother's situation, resisting could be choosing to rationalize, deny, or ignore her reality. But this reaction would not ultimately serve her or cure her. The progression of her dementia was painful to accept, yet it enabled me to access a depth of compassion for her and for its impact on my father, compassion that would have been impossible to muster had I stayed in resistance.

To resist reality takes intentional effort, which can be physically, practically and emotionally costly. Consider something you have resisted to accept. Maybe it is an aspect of your physicality, a relationship that had to end, or like my situation above, the reality of a parent's decline. How much time and effort did you put into fighting it? How did these efforts make you feel? Did your resistance ultimately change anything? If you are like many, your resistance may have consisted of months, or even years of fruitless effort, which ultimately changed nothing and left you feeling frustrated, disempowered, and exhausted.

Acceptance can enable us to put down our fighting gloves and breathe. It can give us space to savor every moment with our parents while they are still with us, to enjoy the parts of our bodies that still function optimally, and to know that every hot flash will pass as quickly as it came on. Once we ease into acceptance, we set the stage to embrace.

To Embrace: An Overview

The term "embrace," as my midlife motto, appeared as quickly and unexpectedly as a hot flash. It was not a word I used with regularity or had any special affinity toward. After that pivotal hot flash, it just popped into my head organically, and felt right, so I went with it. In fact, I did not even look up the definition of the word until

I began to work on this book, which was many years after I started my company, which is also called "Embrace the Middle."

When I did ultimately research the formal definition, I discovered that it essentially pertains to acceptance: "**to embrace:** to accept an idea, a proposal, a set of beliefs, etc., especially when it is done with enthusiasm" (*Oxford Dictionary*).

Rather than stipulating enthusiasm, my definition of what it means to embrace is the following:

> **To embrace** is to accept inevitable midlife changes, challenges, and gifts with presence and compassion.

Acceptance is absolutely part of my conceptualization of embracing. Where my definition differs is the wider, and often more difficult, scope of all that we strive to accept in midlife and *how* we go about it.

In different terms, to embrace is to lean in to midlife, in a gentle, mindful manner. Enthusiasm is great but not everything we confront in the middle decades can be met with enthusiasm. When we accept with presence and compassion, there are no expectations; we notice exactly what is happening, while being gentle with ourselves. If acceptance also calls for action, then we turn to our inner wisdom as our compass. Let's explore this trio—presence, compassion, and wisdom—in more depth.

Presence

Presence is the intentional effort to be with whatever is happening in our lives, whether it is joyful, neutral, or challenging. It is looking life directly in the eye, as opposed to covering our eyes or looking away. Presence is allowing ourselves to feel all of our feelings, including the ones that are uncomfortable, instead of avoiding them. Presence is the ability to refrain from getting lost in thoughts of "why this?" or blame and, alternatively, to remember to tune in to our breath, bodily sensations, and environment. Presence is what I practiced when I had that hot flash.

Over the years, many friends and clients have shared their desire to be more present in their lives. They want to (or think they want to) give their loved ones more attention, have some respite from their constant inner chatter, or even to enjoy a sunset without feeling the anxious pull to go inside to prepare dinner or respond to emails. These desires are often the force that drives people to enroll in one of my workshops, pursue one-to-one mindfulness training with me, or join my meditation group. I "get" it. I am one of these people. Even with decades of meditation practice, I still have to work deliberately to stay present.

Being present, whether to challenges or to good stuff, can feel uncomfortable, anxiety producing, and even vulnerable. Presence goes against our conditioning to be busy and multitask, to incessantly think, and to push away unwanted feelings. We have been rewarded when we got things done, not when we stayed present to challenging situations or moments of discomfort and allowed them to pass.

It might seem that paying more attention to unwanted circumstances, thoughts, and emotions will make us feel worse. Paradoxically, rather than making the situation more challenging, presence allows for perspective, release, and relief, akin to what we feel when we allow our tears to flow. With practice, we realize that it is actually easier to be with the discomfort than it is to exert the effort to run away from challenges. Presence can provide clarity and reveal the truth that thoughts, feelings, and emotions constantly change, if we refrain from actively pushing them away. These are but a few of the many gifts of presence.

So, *how* can we be more present? How do we not get sucked into habitual, automatic ways of reacting, rather than responding, to difficult life circumstances? How do we not run and hide from unwanted experiences or emotions when the compulsion can feel so strong and natural?

Most of us need to learn how to be more present; our minds need to be trained *how* to slow down and stay in the moment. And it takes consistent practice. Meditation is a formal practice of presence—an intentional process whereby we practice staying in the "here and now," using anchors as our aid. Meditative anchors to presence include our breath, bodily sensations, sounds, or even words. Meditation is simple, even though it is sometimes difficult. As we cultivate presence, we bring more of that quality to our day-to-day activities—when we listen to a friend, when we eat a meal, when we see a beautiful cloud formation. Furthermore, we increasingly notice when we are lost in thought or distracting activities.

To this end, the purpose of meditation extends beyond our dedicated meditation time; we practice it "on the cushion," in order to learn how to have more moments of presence in life "off the cushion." With time, we may notice that we are more patient, less reactive, and more attentive to glorious sights and sounds. We increasingly choose how to respond rather than automatically react; how to access choices beyond our instinctual ways of behaving. And the more we hone this skill, the more moments of presence we are able to enjoy in our daily lives.

I remember the first time I vividly experienced the power of presence. It was twenty years ago, during a meditation retreat, which is fitting given that retreats are extended blocks of time dedicated to the practice of being present. This was one of my first retreats, long before the hot flash experience. I was feeling happy and mushy thinking of my then two- and four-year-old daughters and my husband. My body was tingly with joy and my heart felt as if it were exploding with affection at the mere thought of them. I was smiling from ear to ear.

Then, all of a sudden, that delicious experience took a dark turn as my mind began to pose questions: What if something happened to one of them? What if something happened to all three? What if they got into a car accident and I did not know? My smile curved into a frown as panic began to spread through my body. I felt instantly queasy, my heart raced, and beads of sweat formed on my temples. Even though I knew my thoughts were unreasonable, I had an over-whelming compulsion to run out of the meditation hall and call my husband to make sure all was okay.

But I did not get up and call. I committed to sit still, both for my own practice and out of respect for my fellow meditators. I agreed to leave the room only if it was an emergency. Thought-induced panic did not qualify as an emergency. So, I stayed with my visceral experience of anxiety. I turned my attention back to my breath, and paused my catastrophic thinking. My heart rate slowed, my sweating ceased, and the compulsion to call diminished as I had more distance from my imagined scenarios. Many hours later, during our evening break, I called my husband to check on the girls. All was fine on the home front. But staying with my distress in real-time, rather than calling my husband for reassurance hours prior, quelled a panic that my mind had manifested and my body had followed accordingly. It was a rich learning experience of the power of our thoughts and the power of staying present.

Midlife is filled with good stuff and not-so-good stuff; experiences that are delightful and those that are heart-wrenching. Striving to be more present to them all is a tall, courageous invitation, but one that brings with it unexpected freedom and gifts. To be able to see and be with your aging parents or your growing children is a priceless gift that deepens those relationships. To be present to your grief after losing a loved one is to honor the depth of your love and what you shared during your time together. And to be present to the greater certainty and ease that comes with age is a wonderful, yet often missed, gift of midlife.

Presence is the first prong of embracing. The next element—compassion—captures the tone of what it means to embrace.

Compassion

Compassion is the quality of tenderness with which we embrace. It is a deliberate choice to be gentle with ourselves (i.e., self-compassionate) rather than harsh, frustrated, or impatient as we navigate our changing selves and changing lives. Self-compassion means that we give ourselves the same tenderness we so instinctively give to others when we see them struggling and want to ease their pain. To be self-compassionate is to softly acknowledge that caretaking demands, inevitable losses, and our aging bodies are difficult. Self-compassion is being more mindful of our harsh inner narrative and choosing to have a kinder, more realistic self-appraisal.

When I first started to practice self-compassion, I was amazed at how hard I was on myself. Over the years, my husband and teachers had commented on this tendency, but I had consistently responded with a dismissive, "Yeah, I know." In truth, I did *not* know the extent of my self-criticism until I made an intentional effort to notice. To my dismay, my inner critic (that judgmental voice in my head) seemed to work twenty-four hours a day, seven days a week, spewing out a steady stream of criticism: "I'm so disorganized," "I'm a bad cook," "I look awful in this," and, in my darkest hours, "I have not done anything of significance in my life." It never ended.

Furthermore, I seldom acknowledged my accomplishments or amiable qualities, such as my big heart and kind nature. I downplayed my doctorate ("It's only in psychology"), my workshop accolades ("But you women did all the work!"), and my parenting kudos ("It's not me. I am blessed with amazing daughters). I noticed how often "I hate," "I should," and "I'm sorry," were in my verbal repertoire. And as I aged, the list of things to downplay, judge, and reject seemed to grow exponentially.

I also became aware of the longer-term impact of my harsh self-judgment. Even when my responses to compliments were a form of false modesty, and I knew my self-criticisms were not entirely true, they collectively and steadily chipped away at my sense of self and power. "I hate my belly," was saying, "I hate a part of myself." My belly is not disconnected from me; it is an intrinsic part of me.

Awareness of how hard I was on myself was the first step. With that awareness, I gradually lessened my automatic self-critical thoughts and narrative. I can now more easily catch myself when they try to take over, and I am able to refrain from indulging in these thoughts with greater ease. My inner critic is still there, but she is much quieter and more subdued. And when she raises her voice, I can choose whether or not I want to listen to her chatter or join her.

A few years ago, my skin started to change. I would bleed at the slightest scratch and the wound would spread, forming dark purple bruises that would last for weeks. One particularly large spot on my leg would not fade. It is still there. My arms looked like my parents' arms when they were in their eighties and on blood thinners. But I was in my fifties and not on any medication associated with bruising. I hated the way it looked.

I went to five different dermatologists and emailed an encyclopedia of pictures of these recurring bruises, adamant that something was wrong. I was certain I had a deficiency or a dermatological condition that could be treated with a medication or cream. But that was not the case. It was a condition called solar purpura, which is essentially thinning skin due to aging and sun damage. Nothing could treat it. The recommendation was prevention by wearing long sleeves and pants and staying out of the sun.

That was not going to work. I live in Southern California, love the outdoors, and have a post-menopausal inner thermostat. I am always warm and most always in tank tops. I was uncomfortable even at the thought of wearing long sleeves. And, until these ugly bruises appeared, I actually liked my arms. I did not want to accept this was my reality. I Googled incessantly, hoping to find some unknown cure. I consulted with aestheticians, applied bruising creams, and tried supplements, all to no avail. Nothing helped. That is, nothing except one thing: self-compassion.

It helped when I stopped trying to fix the unfixable and appreciated how incredibly difficult this was for me. It helped when I began to take better care of my arms by diligently and gently applying sunscreen and being more mindful not to get scratched. I still do not like the condition but I accept that this is an aspect of my aging process and ceased looking at my arms with disdain. I continue to apply bruising creams and sometimes even cover-up makeup, but I do so with love.

One of the senior students at my Zen center, an Australian woman, often included the words "bring gentle awareness" in her student talks. For years, I could not understand what she meant by gentle awareness. It sounded lovely, especially in her Australian accent, but I had no clue how to actually make my awareness gentle. For me, awareness was awareness. Period.

And then one day, many years later, I got it in one of those "aha" experiences. The understanding came as I was practicing awareness of my experience of anxiety. I was struggling to stay present to intense rippling sensations in my belly and constriction in my throat. I realized that the quality of my attention did not have to be equally intense; rather than noticing these bodily sensations in the blinding light of midday, I could see them in the softer, golden light of sunset. I immediately felt a shift. With that, I switched my self-talk from

"Here are those awful twinges of lightning bolts rippling through my body" to "Oh…this is what anxiety feels like." I got it; that was what my friend meant by gentle presence. The subtle shift made a profound difference.

Today, when a scratch on my arm rapidly forms into a purple bruise, I try to gently look at it and say, "My poor arms…there's another bruise and I apply arnica," rather than "Shit, another nasty bruise for two weeks!" This is gentle awareness. It is a difficult concept to explain in words but one that I can assure you will understand when your awareness lens shifts from "Aargh…" to "Aah…" Nothing is different about the situation except your compassionate response.

There are so many moments, passages, and transitions in mid-life that call for gentleness. When we treat our bodies, our memory lapses, our endings, our beginnings, and our in-between states with tenderness, it can transform the experiences and, in turn, the quality of our lives. We just have to remember to do it.

At my local Zen center, we end our sitting practice with a closing verse. This is the final line:

"Each moment, life as it is, the only teacher. Being
just this moment, compassion's way."

Sometimes, presence and compassion are sufficient. Our soft acceptance is enough to manage the moment with more ease. Other times, the situation may call for action. In those cases, we turn to something inherent in women in the middle decades: wisdom.

Wisdom

Wisdom is defined as "the quality of having experience, knowledge, and good judgment" (*Oxford Dictionary*). It is more than a collection of facts or information. Wisdom is the lessons we can derive from reflecting on our varied life experiences. Over time, we may begin to see patterns and connections that were previously unnoticed, allowing us to make decisions and view life with a broader, more informed perspective. This is the essence of wisdom—an ever-evolving collection of insights that can impact our outlook, choices, and judgment.

There is absolutely a relationship between age and wisdom, which I address in Chapter 7. However, I maintain that wisdom is not merely a function of living longer. It also relates to the richness of the experiences we encounter by virtue of age, such as losses, illnesses, or big successes, and how we choose to relate to them and move forward. Wisdom grows from both the breadth and depth of our life experiences. When we listen to our wisdom, it can help us navigate the complexities of life with greater ease, understand deeper truths, and make decisions from both our head and heart.

Sometimes, in the hustle and bustle of daily life, and particularly during stressful times, we can forget our accumulated wisdom. We may find ourselves reacting to situations with the urgency of the moment or thinking, "I have no idea what to do" or "How will I ever get through this?" In the moment, these thoughts feel real, and may sometimes be true. But more often, our depth of despair or urge to do something right now obscures our access to our wisdom. This wisdom is not lost; it lives within us, woven into the very fabric of our being. When we take the time to pause, reflect, and listen, our wisdom can surface. I explore wisdom in more depth in Chapter 7, as it is also the number one gift of midlife for this research sample.

To embrace is to consciously tune in to our inner wisdom. To embrace is to intentionally draw upon the decades of life lessons we have earned and own. Presence and compassion set the stage and aid our ability to "tune in" and retrieve our individual wisdom.

A legendary Chinese Taoist philosopher, Lao Tzu, once stated: "At the center of your being you have the answer. You know who you are. You know what you want." I agree.

Examples of Embracing

While I have referenced my experiences to illustrate embracing, I have gleaned many other examples from the women in the research, and from attendees of my workshops. Here are three examples of times when women chose to embrace their midlife passages.

Gayle's decision to embrace her body manifested when she finally gave away her "skinny jeans"—her symbol of her desired younger body. Despite having a stable weight for years, she clung onto her "skinny jeans" in hopes that someday she would again fit into their smaller size and, as a result, like her body. But each time she tried to wiggle into them, her self-worth plummeted and her inner critic pounced. Gayle finally decided to toss the jeans, relinquish their power over her self-esteem, and tenderly accept her more mature figure (and realistic jeans size). She was amazed at the impact of that small, but highly symbolic, step in paving the way toward gentle self-acceptance.

A few months after Russia invaded Ukraine, Anna's twenty-year-old son announced his intention to quit his job as a telemarketer and volunteer with the Ukrainian armed services. His grandparents had emigrated from Ukraine, he was devastated by the situation, and he was adamant to help. As you might expect, Anna questioned his choice and feared for his well-being. Yet, she disciplined herself to embrace this reality and not try to convince him otherwise. Anna was present to her sorrow and fear, and ultimately accepted and blessed his decision. She was tender toward her aching heart while appreciating the necessity of allowing her son to follow his own big heart.

Alex's decision to divorce her husband was a courageous and self-loving embrace of her marital reality. "I know everyone thought my husband was great but that's not who he was at home. He is not a nice man. I had to divorce him out of self-respect. And I needed to model to my kids that they cannot allow a man to treat a woman like my ex-husband treated me. It was really hard, and my mom didn't support it in the beginning, but I found my power and got myself back in the process."

Gayle, Anna, and Alex courageously moved toward their midlife junctures. They were tenderly present to their sadness, fear, and vulnerability. And by doing so, they moved through these changes with grace and discovered new degrees of strength. By choosing not to fight battles they could not win, and to listen to their hearts, they felt freer and more empowered.

While I was writing this book, a movie titled *Good Luck to You, Leo Grande*, starring Emma Thompson, was released. The scene I had heard the most about was one in which Emma, at age sixty-five, is entirely nude. In interviews, she shared how difficult and vulnerable it was for her to shoot that segment.

Emma's character is a sixty-something, sexually repressed widow who hires a sex worker, Leo, to help her complete a checklist of sexual ventures. In an early scene in the movie, Emma is standing fully clothed in front of a full-length mirror, reluctantly looking at her body. Her facial expression is disdainful as she hurriedly hones in on her many dislikes before looking away.

Much happens over the course of the movie but it is the very last scene that is so compelling to me. Emma's character, having emotionally evolved, again stands before a full-length mirror but nude instead of clothed. As she takes in her body this time, with full presence, a gentle smile of love and acceptance forms. The scene closes with a close-up on her face, which has transformed from contempt to a soft, almost angelic-looking expression. That is a moment of embracing.

The Bottom Line

To embrace is an approach to midlife that beckons presence and compassion, and uses our earned wisdom to navigate our changing selves and lives. It is learning to gently lean in to life and fully accept our reality, even when we would rather cover our eyes or run away.

To resist, which many of us habitually do, is the opposite of embracing. It is to refuse to accept our reality or try to prevent inevitable changes. Though the instinct to resist may be natural, doing so diminishes our life, and is physically and emotionally exhausting. The essence of this book is an invitation to embrace the myriad changes that abound in midlife.

In the following chapter, I will explain the nature of my research, share the impetus for the study, and introduce you to some of the many women who are a part of it.

CHAPTER 2

THANKS FOR ASKING

"It took me quite a long time to develop a voice, and now that I have it, I am not going to be silent."

—Madeleine Albright

It was the afternoon of Wednesday, March 11, 2020. I was in a checkout line at Target with a twelve-pack of coveted toilet paper in my hands when my phone started to blow up with incoming text messages. All wanted to know the whereabouts of my nineteen-year-old daughter Tara, who was halfway around the world in France, working as an au pair.

I froze in fear, as my heart instantly began to race and the color drained from my face. Had something happened in France, or to Tara, and I was the last to know? I was momentarily paralyzed. "Breathe," I told myself.

A few seconds later, Jerry, my next-door neighbor, called.

"What's wrong?" I answered.

"Have you been watching television?" he asked.

"No," I replied, "I'm in Target." (As if that mattered.)

"You'd better go turn it on. The president just ordered the borders to close in two days. You might want to get Tara home."

Anxiety and dread began to wash over me. That same Friday was to be her last day of work and the beginning of her two months of travel—what she had planned and worked for all year long. She was going to be devastated. And the pandemic was clearly spreading. My husband was also overseas, in Sri Lanka, on business. I had to get them home.

The next twenty-four hours were an anxiety-filled blur. I tried to book Tara on flights that were selling out before my eyes, while my husband was working his way home through three different countries while feeling unwell (not COVID, but definitely ill). I was up all night in order to track each of their flights, and would exhale whenever they made it out of a different country. Fortunately, they both made it home, unlike a few of Tara's fellow au pairs, who ended up getting stuck in France.

Little did any of us know that this was the beginning of one of the most surreal chapters of our lives. With the onset of the pandemic, the world as we all knew it abruptly stopped. The "Big Pause" was one of the more positive descriptors. That was an understatement.

I took advantage of the unexpected COVID-related free time to research the experiences of women in midlife. At the time, my company Embrace the Middle was relatively new. And, in my mid-fifties, I still felt new to midlife. Despite being squarely in the middle chronologically, it was only recently that I felt my age—first when my mom died, and the following year when Tara moved to Europe. I was actively trying to navigate a world without my mother alive, or my oldest child living at home.

I also knew of significant changes happening in the worlds of my friends and clients. In recent years, women in my immediate circle have faced cancer, infidelity, divorce, existential crises, and challenging menopausal symptoms—as well as good stuff like career advances, growing confidence, new relationships, and finally putting their own needs at the forefront.

And, I wanted a wider sample. I hoped to gain a deeper under-standing of us, our lives, and our needs. I wondered if there were universal aspects to being a woman in midlife or if our individuality meant we would have unique midlife experiences as well.

On a personal level, I was curious how my midlife experience compared with others.

How were other women impacted by their mothers' deaths? Did women find the empty nest to be liberating, depressing, or both? And was I the only one who thought perimenopause, which no one discussed when I went through it, was far more challenging than menopause?

Perimenopause means "around menopause." It is the transitional period between a woman's peak reproductive years and menopause, when fertility ends. Because of hormonal fluctuations, many women experience symptoms more commonly associated with menopause during perimenopause. Some of these symptoms include hot flashes, sleep disturbances, anxiety, heart palpitations, and vaginal dryness.

Menopause is when women permanently stop having menstrual periods. It is confirmed when a woman has not had her period for twelve consecutive months. Some symptoms associated with menopause can (but don't always) include hot flashes, night sweats, sleep disturbances, emotional challenges, vaginal dryness, heart palpitations, changes in libido, memory lapses, weight gain, and hair loss or thinning.

To get more information on these questions, I created a survey which addressed the following areas:

* Midlife Challenges
* Midlife Gifts
* Helpful Tools (in navigating the challenges)

I sent the survey to around thirty-five friends and colleagues and posted it on a few social media sites. With the survey came the gentle request to "feel free to share with your female friends in midlife." I also asked a few well-connected women in my circles to share it with their networks. My goal was to survey approximately one hundred women. To my surprise and delight, the survey spread like wildfire. Not only were women across the United States completing it, but somehow it reached women internationally as well.

By the time I closed the survey, at the end of 2020, I had 619 respondents. Most every continent was represented, with close to one hundred of the women residing in Europe. The data not only captured the experience of a significant sample of midlife women, but it also shed light on whether there are cultural variations to the midlife experience, or if this time of our lives transcends unique cultures.[1]

Beyond the survey responses, I decided to continue this midlife inquiry on a deeper level, an idea that emerged while hiking with a girlfriend. As my friend and I were discussing the survey, I asked her to explain why she felt that "sandwich" demands (i.e., the concurrent needs of our kids and parents/parents-in-law) are especially challenging. Her unexpected response was something like this: "Because my mom and daughter both need me more and more and I cannot be there enough for either of them. Work is so demanding that I had to

---

[1]   See Appendix 2.

hire someone to take my mom to her many doctors' appointments and record what the doctors say. Ilana (her daughter) won't explain her moods, and I had to hire a dog walker so that I can drive Ilana to school. I do the best I can but still feel guilty that I am missing out on so much important stuff. And if I ask to take time off to do these things, I might as well put in a resignation notice. I'd get one of those judgmental stares, and a younger version of me would jump at the opportunity to take over my job."

I was in pain for my friend. She was conflicted and guilt-ridden due the competing demands on her time. She had worked at the same company for decades, loved it, and was on track to become its Chief Financial Officer (CFO).

And wow! Her experience was so different from mine. I too had sandwich stressors but for entirely different reasons. Being self-employed, I had the flexibility to tend to the needs of my daughters, my in-laws, and my medically challenged dog, but admittedly sometimes resented that it took time away from work—and that my business growth was slower as a result. It was a chosen trade-off but a trade-off, nonetheless. In fact, I only found the physical and mental space to start writing this book after my younger daughter left for university.

From this conversation with my friend, I realized that a response to a survey question (i.e., to mark "very challenged" with regards to sandwich demands) could not sufficiently capture the variety of midlife experiences behind the answer to the question. Though my friend and I were both challenged by multigenerational demands, our situations were entirely different.

The different ways women were impacted by similar challenges was something that came up repeatedly in the research. That is, women in midlife have many similar experiences. At some point, if we haven't already, we will all enter menopause, lose a loved one, and experience some aspect of physical decline. Yet, there is tremendous variability in terms of when and how these difficulties appear, the way we manage them, and the degree to which they impact our lives. Our experience of, and response to, our challenges are influenced by our histories, resources, attitudes, and life circumstances.

So, on that same hike, I decided to dive deeper into the research and interview a subset of 100 of the 619 women who completed the survey. I met my goal. In fact, I interviewed 103 amazing women.

And these were not just quick and cursory interviews. These were intimate, honest, hourlong conversations about the hardships and joys of being a woman in midlife.

The interviews were also an opportunity to ask these additional questions:

* ❋ Do you relate to the term "middle age" or "midlife"?
* ❋ What are your defining moments or experiences of midlife?
* ❋ What wisdom would you impart from your midlife lens?
* ❋ What books or authors have helped you manage these years?

Every single interview was compelling. What equally fascinated and perplexed me was, *why* would so many women in midlife choose to participate in these personal interviews? I learned the answer to this question in the course of dinner with my husband and two other couples.

Thanks for Asking

"Why," I said to my friends, "would busy women volunteer to take an hour out of their day (or often evening for women living in different countries) to discuss their personal lives with a stranger?" Since we didn't have a previous relationship and I wasn't compensating them, they must have had another reason to say yes. Sara, one of the women at dinner, looked me squarely in the eyes and said, "It's because you asked." "What do you mean?" I replied. "It's because you asked," she repeated.

Sara then explained her experience and perspective, which I came to learn was shared by many other women in the study: People perceive women in midlife to be less interesting, and erroneously assume we have less to offer, than women in the younger and older decades. We are past the exciting "up and coming" age and have not yet reached the status of the revered elder—the crone. More and more frequently, people stop asking us about ourselves and our thoughts.

Intrigued by Sara's explanation, I started to ask women why they chose to be interviewed. Claudia shared that she works full time and tends to the competing demands of four generations of family members: her parents, grandparents, children, and grandchildren. She explained that she "made the time" to talk with me as the interview was a rare opportunity for her to be the focus of attention. This theme was echoed by others, including Barbi who said, "It was nice to speak about me for a change."

Monique shared that she was motivated to be interviewed because the survey questions illuminated how much she has grown over the years and she was excited to talk to someone who was genuinely interested in her individual journey.

Other women said that they decided to participate because they felt the topic is incredibly important yet wildly overlooked—a bit like us. Rina remarked, "I am honored that someone is looking at us. We are not the Twitter demographic." Avery said that although she is a "private person," she volunteered for the interview in order to be of service to other women. Desiree stated that her menopausal experience was "horrible" and that she wanted to share it, and her indirect path to "life-changing" treatment, in hopes that other women would not have to suffer the way she did.

Every one of the 103 women interviewed had a lot to say and were eager to say it. They were forthcoming about the ups and downs of midlife, including the many different ways they navigate it (e.g., exercise, time in nature, talking with friends, hormone replacement therapy, wine, etc.), and were happy to share their wisdom. They just needed to be asked.

The Research Sample

By the end of December 2020, I had interviewed women from Amsterdam, Brisbane, Brussels, Cartagena, Cologne, Cuenca, Geneva, Haifa, Johannesburg, Luxembourg, Lisbon, Paris, Tel Aviv, Toronto, and from every region in the United States. I loved the many different accents and cultural nuances. I was thrilled when there was a window behind an interviewee, and I knew I was looking at the streets of New York, Paris, or Tel Aviv. On several occasions, I was drinking coffee while the women in Europe were sipping wine (and once, admittedly, vice versa). The biggest time difference was eighteen hours when I interviewed a college sorority sister, currently living in Australia, whom I had not spoken with in over thirty years.

I spent months reliving my doctoral dissertation days as I coded the answers from the recorded interviews into qualitative categorical data. I employed a second person to independently code in order to ensure reliability of our categories. And, I had the wealth of accompanying quantifiable data from the many more women who completed the survey.

The demographic makeup of the 619 survey takers is as follows:

Age: Women from their thirties to their seventies participated in the research. However, the overwhelming majority (91%) of the survey takers were between forty and sixty-nine, with the majority

(42%) of the women being in their fifties. Because relatively few women in their thirties and seventies completed the survey, I ultimately excluded them from the analyses, in order to more accurately capture the experiences of women in their forties, fifties, and sixties.

Marital Status: Most of the women are married (71%), followed by divorced (12%), never married (9%), widowed (5%), and dating (3%).

Work Status: Half of the respondents work full time, followed by 15% who are self-employed, and an additional 15% who are retired. A total of 11% work part time, 7% are caretakers, and 3% are looking for work.

Ethnicity: Because I did not originally design the survey to be a research study, I did not, unfortunately, gather information on ethnicity. However, I made a concerted effort to enroll as ethnically diverse a sample as I could. That being said, my best guesstimate is that between 50% and 60% of the respondents are Caucasian, with the remaining women constituting a diversity of ethnic backgrounds.

Country of Residence: I only started asking the women's country of residence halfway into the data-collection process, when the survey organically spread across the globe. Of the 302 women who identified their residence, 165 live in North America, 95 in the European Union, 17 in Asia, 3 in South America, 10 in Australia, and 2 in Africa.

Professions: The women I interviewed represented a wide variety of vocations. There was more than one woman who worked in the following professions: attorneys, business owners, chief executive officers, coaches, corporate executives, flight attendants, hairdressers, psychologists, medical doctors, and teachers.

Other professions include accountant, aesthetician, art therapist, artist, birth doula, childbirth educator, clairvoyant, college professor, controller, corporate trainer, dance instructor, director of communications, dog trainer, editor, event planner, finance professional, human resource administrator, journalist, lactation specialist, marketer, mikvah attendant, nutritionist, real estate saleswoman, school board executive, school principal, social worker, software designer, tutor, personal trainer, photographer, writer, and yoga teacher.

What an extraordinary, diverse, interesting group of women! It was such a gift to interview each one. They brought me into their homes (usually via Zoom), hearts, and minds, and shared personal and intimate aspects of their lives. I was honored to have their trust and learned so very much from them. Their answers, experiences, and wisdom are more than a significant component of this book. They also motivated me to persevere with my writing in order to tell their stories. Although I share names throughout this book, they have all been changed in order to protect the identity of the interviewees.

My hunch, and hope, is that you will relate to many of the women's stories. And that you will feel seen, heard, and understood as a result.

The Bottom Line

I am not sure if I should thank COVID for giving me the opportunity to do this research or thank the research for keeping me busy during those first surreal months. Either way, the chance to learn more about us was a rich silver lining.

My study consisted of survey responses from 619 midlife women worldwide, which focused on the challenges and gifts of the middle decades. In follow-up interviews, with a subset of 103 diverse women, I explored their survey answers more deeply and had the opportunity to ask additional questions relative to midlife terminology, defining moments, helpful books, and their age-related wisdom. Their answers and stories are shared throughout this book and shed a bright light on what aspects of midlife are most calling to be embraced.

But before I share the survey and interview findings, let's define what I mean by "the middle"—a term, you will learn, that is not easily defined.

CHAPTER 3

WHAT THE HECK IS *THE MIDDLE?*

"Age is simply the number of years the world has been enjoying you."

— Author Unknown

"So, what is the middle?" is a question I'm frequently asked—a fair inquiry given the name of my company and this book. And though this question is seemingly straightforward, the answer is not so clear-cut. As you will read in subsequent pages, it is more nuanced than a precise age range.

Determining where we are in relation to middle age—whether we identify ourselves as not yet there, in its midst, or on the other side of midlife—can influence how we emotionally interpret, and consequently approach, this stage of our lives. For some, the label of middle age beckons descriptors such as "in one's prime" or "ripe" to "mature" or "matronly," all of which can impact our narrative and behavior. Many women in the younger generations, who inquired about the parameters of "the middle," hoped that they were not yet considered middle-aged; they wanted to be adult but not *that* adult.

In contrast, several women in the older decades who were curious to know what constitutes midlife wished they were still considered middle-aged. In their minds, midlife buys them more hope and time. The eagerness of the questioners, while awaiting my answer, illustrates the power of language.

At the end of this chapter, I will propose a definition of the middle. But in order to do so, it is important to understand the complexities of answering the simple question of what constitutes "the middle."

Is it a number?

Most people who ask about the definition of midlife expect to hear an age range. Frankly, when I started working with women in this demographic, I, too, was focused on naming a numerical range to encapsulate "the middle." Research has found that the majority of people consider midlife to fall somewhere within the forties and sixties. I, too, considered the forties, fifties, and possibly sixties to be middle age. Because I married and had kids well into my thirties, I personally could not connect with that decade as being part of the middle. I still had an infant when I was thirty-eight! But I definitely felt more mature in my forties and fifties. There were clear shifts in my identity, life, and perspective that reflected more years of life experience.

I was less clear about the sixties. The sixties are certainly not old age. I believe this now more than ever, as I rapidly approach sixty. Yet this decade is very different from the forties and fifties. Life decisions, such as when and how to retire, and circumstances, such as the entry of grandchildren for some, emerge. And society views the sixties differently, as exemplified by mandated retirement in certain professions and various governmental and societal benefits awarded when we reach sixty-five. I have begun to consider the mid to upper sixties as a liminal period, between the middle and senior years.

Though all three decades, as well as the mid to latter thirties, can be considered middle age, the aspects of midlife that we face within each of those decades can vary. This made me consider that there are different parts to the middle: an early middle, a middle middle, and a later middle. Or perhaps it is all a liminal period.

In some ways, we are always in the middle—between birth and death. At any age, we have no way of knowing how many days or decades we may have ahead. This was painfully reinforced when my brother Eddie passed away quite unexpectedly at the young age of sixty. Sadly, Eddie's midlife years ended up being between twenty and forty. So, with all of these nuances, age became an increasingly insufficient way to define midlife.

Is it milestones?

Perhaps "the middle" is more accurately represented by when we experience certain defining life milestones, such as menopause or when our parents pass. The former marks the end of the possibility of bearing children, which has significant practical and emotional implications.

Our parents' passing can drive home our indisputable adulthood and prompt us to come face-to-face with our own mortality. I felt undeniably more adult, and viewed life differently, once I went through both of these milestones, which happened in my fifties. Both profoundly shook my foundation and upended my developmental perspective. There was no disputing I had entered a different, more mature season of life.

However, some women experience these defining milestones in earlier decades. For example, a few women I interviewed had children or lost a parent in their teen years, catapulting them into a more advanced developmental season. Their responsibilities and perspective, at tender ages, became more akin to what many of us first experience in middle decades. So, using milestones to define midlife is also problematic.

Or is it our life lens?

I also wondered whether midlife could be best defined by our shifting, more-mature lens. Perhaps it is when we are able to ground our life lessons into wisdom, which we then increasingly use to guide our choices and behavior. Maybe it is when we become less self-focused—and more aware, more conscious, and more connected to the wider world in which we live. Alternatively, is it when we settle more easily into a "being" mindset as opposed to a predominantly "doing" mindset? Or is it as simple as our attitude toward aging?

I ultimately concluded that midlife is a combination of them all: when we reach certain ages, when we have pivotal life experiences, and definitely when our perspective widens and matures.

After sharing what other women have to say about midlife, I will offer my definition of "the middle." But for now, read on to learn the many different ways the interviewees capture and define midlife.

Interview Question 1: Do you relate to the terms "middle age" or "midlife"?

By and large, No

If there is one thing virtually every woman I interviewed agreed upon, it was a dislike of (and even disdain for) the term "middle age." The majority felt the term should be retired as a descriptor for these decades. It was overwhelmingly perceived as pejorative, archaic, and connoting decline. Additionally, its exclusive reference to a number does not capture the many other considerations described above.

More women connected with the term "midlife," though they did not love it. They usually paused when asked if they related to this term, not automatically rejecting it like they did "middle age," but not unequivocally aligning with it either.

"Midlife" is softer than "middle age" but still not warm or inviting, like the "golden years," a term often associated with subsequent decades. It also brings to mind the deeply ingrained association with the word "crisis," a stereotype implying that people can behave in desperate ways in order to defy their aging. Although there are many changes happening in the middle decade, *not one woman I spoke with described herself as being in crisis.* Existential reckoning, contemplation, and transition are more fitting descriptors.

In her book, *The Queen of Myself,* Donna Henes captured the crossroads of midlife as "an overwhelming crisis of identity and purposes." We may experience crisis in certain aspects of our lives, but not in the way "midlife crisis" has historically implied. In sum, the term "midlife" is limiting, narrow, and negatively associated with the word "crisis."

Unlike the terms "middle age" and "midlife," considering these decades as a different season was highly resonant.

Interview Question 2: Do you relate to being in a different season of your life?

Yes, for most

When responding to this question, the overwhelming majority of the women replied, "Yes!" "Absolutely," and "Definitely!" And those exclamation points are intentional. They reflect the certainty women conveyed in their answers. The concept of being in a "season" more fully captures the myriad moving parts and changes inherent in midlife that extend beyond our age.

I followed up this question by asking the interviewees if they had a specific term to describe this season of their lives. Here's how some of the women responded:

It's a Season of _____

* Arrival
* Authenticity
* Becoming
* Being
* Chaos
* Curiosity
* Difficulties
* Empowerment
* Excitement
* Invisibility
* Liminality
* Living and Assessing Life Concurrently
* Purpose
* Seeing More Clearly
* Transitions
* Unfolding
* Waking Up

And the colorful, "A humorous reckoning with the downhill deterioration."

I love these descriptors. And to every single one, I nodded and replied, "Absolutely." Midlife is about all of those aspects.

These illuminating and sometimes seemingly contradictory terms capture the vast tapestry of the season. It is exciting *and* it is difficult.

We do "see more" *and* yet are "seen less." And we are "waking up" at the same time as we are "deteriorating." There is a lot going on, all at the same time.

Other Midlife Descriptors

Even though all of us appreciate that there is a gamut of midlife experiences, not all women relate to the idea of midlife being captured as a categorically different season.

Some women view midlife as part of the continuum of life, another year, or in Marni's words, "The next adventure." Lili said, "I see myself on a timeline that stretches backward and forward." Elizabeth believes "It's not a number or season; it's the nuances of when you begin to wake up."

Others viewed life as being composed of phases, quarters, thirds, halves, and to one, seven-year cycles. I can relate to that last one. From that perspective, I am in a new cycle—and feel it.

Carl Jung, the brilliant psychologist, agreed with this take on midlife. He conceptualized midlife as "the afternoon of life," a critical period linking the morning (earlier) and the evening (later) periods.

Nancy's response that "age is entirely a state of mind" captures the concept of age identity, a term proposed by Erving Goffman, a Canadian-American sociologist. According to Goffman, age-identity refers to "the inner experience of a person's age and aging process."[2] It is our subjective experience of our age.

The related saying, "You're only as old as you feel," also falls in this realm. The extensive study on Midlife Development in the United States (MIDUS),[3] conducted by the National Institute of

---

[2]   Goffman E. *The Presentation of Self in Everyday Life* (Garden City, NY: Doubleday Anchor Books. 1963).

[3]   www.Midus.Wisc.edu.

Health, and other researchers,[4] found that overall, the gap between one's actual age and perceived age increases over time beginning at age thirty. Meaning, at forty, we may feel as if we are thirty-five, whereas at fifty, we may perceive our age to be forty. For healthy people, the gap grows with age. That is encouraging data.

Defining Moments

I also asked my interviewees if there were any personal experiences or moments that were defining, relative to midlife. A defining moment can be just that—a moment in time that yields a dramatic change, such as when a child is born or a loved one dies. It is that instant when your world as you knew it is measurably different.

A defining moment can also be more gradual—not an instant, but rather a period—such as when we find ourselves calm in situations that historically upended us, or when we laugh at an error rather than beat ourselves up over it. As one woman succinctly said, "It's not a singular experience; it's a process of adulting more than moments." So, with that backdrop, here are some of the women's responses.

Question 3: Do you have any midlife milestones or defining moments?

Absolutely!

The themes women shared around defining moments are those that will continue to resurface in other contexts: loss, physical decline,

---

4   Westerhof, G.J. "Age Identity." In D. Carr (Ed.), *Encyclopedia of the Life Course and Human Development.* Vol 3: 10–14. (Farmington Hills, MI: Macmillan, 2008).

reaching menopause, increased power, invisibility, and shifts in perspective. Consider these examples.

San described an incident when she fainted and fell as she was getting out of her jacuzzi. She sustained a mild head injury and three bruised ribs. She eventually recovered from her injuries but the psychological insult and vulnerability of it stayed with her. Hot tubbing, a gentle activity, was frequently part of her day. To feel physically unstable from that everyday activity shook her world. Her body was no longer a rock she could trust.

Sarah was offered an unexpected promotion, which came with much more responsibility, including overseeing a team of twelve, an increase of ten people from her current position. During the meeting with her boss where she was offered the promotion, she surprised herself when she immediately replied, "Yes, thank you." Gone was her historical hesitation due to doubt in her competence and fear of not being perfect. She knew she would face a steep learning curve, and make mistakes along the way, and that was okay. Her awareness of how far she had grown emotionally, as exemplified by her immediate "yes," was huge. And an absolute defining moment.

Ari, now fifty-two, had a hysterectomy in her early thirties. Not only did that mean the end of her dream of bearing children but it also put her into instant menopause. "I had no idea it would be like this. I felt like I went into the surgery as a young adult and came out of it a middle-aged woman."

Countless women echoed the defining experience of looking in the mirror and being taken aback by the older woman in the reflection. "Is that really me?" "I don't feel as old as that woman looks," were typical reactions.

Describing Midlife in Their Own Words

Consistent with the many different ways women define and connect with midlife, these quotes illustrate the diversity of our experience of age:

* ❋ "I started referring to myself as middle-age at thirty-five. I like the idea of being settled (age 40)."
* ❋ "I just started the second half and am excited where it will take me (age 42)."
* ❋ "I like that I'm in the middle: It tells me I can still do a lot (44)."
* ❋ "I'm fighting it. I'm resentful (45)."
* ❋ "In two words, everything's better (46)."
* ❋ "It's really hard. Menopause is killing me (47)."
* ❋ "I'm having a great time; can't relate to the crisis thing at all (48)."
* ❋ "I'm softening into a genuine appreciation of myself and others (49)."
* ❋ "Fifty is downright magical (50)."
* ❋ "It's my most exciting time yet (51)."
* ❋ "It seems we become wiser and more authentic as we age (52)."
* ❋ "It's utterly lacking in joy, especially the sex (53)."
* ❋ "I am gentler with myself (54)."
* ❋ "I am shocked when I say my age (57)."
* ❋ "The older I am, the better life is (58)."
* ❋ "I have a twenty-year-old so I don't feel old at all (61)."
* ❋ "I'm honored by my age (65)."

At age sixty, Oprah said, "The way I see it, every year can be a brand-new journey. Think about it: You get one chance to be 25, 38, 44, 61, and every age before and between. Why wouldn't you want to experience all the wonder in each step on your path?"

That opening question, "What is the middle?" is not so simple to answer. It took several pages to address, within which were many different opinions. Dr. Marjorie Lachman, a psychologist, researcher, and expert on midlife, spoke to the significance of all of these aspects when she wrote, "More important for defining midlife than chronological age are the unique role constellations that people take on combined with the timing of life events and experiences."[5] Based on results from the MIDUS study, Lachman and her fellow researchers concluded: "We present middle age as a pivotal period in the life course in terms of balancing growth and decline, linking earlier and later periods of life, and bridging younger and older generations."[6] Based on my research, I define the middle as follows:

> **The middle** is a transformational season, typically between one's forties and sixties, which is marked by growth, decline, empowerment, and loss, and experienced with amplified wisdom, self-awareness, and agency.

---

[5] Lachman, ME. "Development in Midlife." *Annual Review of Psychology.* 2004 55: 305–31.

[6] Lachman ME, Teshale S., Agrigoroaei S. "Midlife as a Pivotal Period in the Life Course: Balancing Growth and Decline at the Crossroads of Youth and Old Age." *International Journal of Behavioral Development.* 2015 39 (1).

The Bottom Line

What you consider to be "the middle" is personal, drawn from your unique history, perspective, and current circumstances. Clearly, your chronological age is one aspect, but it is also how and when you experience certain milestones, challenges, and emotional growth. It is how and when you are faced with increasing "adult" responsibilities and the awareness of decreasing time. It is how and when you step into your adult shoes, lace them up, and begin to walk in them. And, it is how and when you begin to see life through a more nuanced and mature lens.

Now that I have defined "embracing" and "the middle," let's explore *how* we combine them. The next chapter explains my step-by-step process to embrace the middle—to bring more presence, compassion, and wisdom into the many components of midlife.

CHAPTER 4

INTRODUCING SOFTT

"Be soft. Do not let the world make you hard. Do not let pain make you hate. Do not let bitterness steal your sweetness."

—Kurt Vonnegut, Jr.

A few weeks ago, my Tuesday morning started out as a mindless routine. I gulped down a cup of coffee and proceeded to mechanically wash my face and hurriedly slap on some moisturizer. I brushed my teeth like a machine, and then threw on a pair of leggings, only to immediately toss them aside in favor of another pair. I became aware of the quality of my actions ten minutes later, when I realized that I was aggressively scrubbing my empty coffee mug. All it had in it was liquids! I didn't need to wash it with such intensity.

The paradox of my rough morning of "self-care" was not lost on me. I barely tasted my coffee and had practically chafed my skin with cream intended to moisten it. At that moment, I set an intention to be softer in my daily rituals: to slowly enjoy my coffee, to be gentler with my skin and teeth, and to take a minute to neatly fold my discarded clothing (well, most of the time).

So much of midlife, far beyond our self-care rituals, would benefit from softness. Many of the changes common during the middle decades are difficult. Furthermore, these challenging life transitions occur amidst a harsh midlife social climate—demeaning stereotypes, cultures awash in ageism and sexism, and a decrease in our visibility.

To compound matters, amidst these myriad challenges, there continues to be a habitual pattern for many of us to treat ourselves unkindly. We can criticize our changing appearance, get angry with our bodies for their diminishing abilities, or beat ourselves up for losing patience with our elders. These reactions are understandable; difficult life circumstances breed edginess, not gentleness. But harsh judgments like these only add to our suffering. We need tenderness, not self-criticism.

I will delve deeply into the personal and cultural midlife challenges in subsequent chapters. But, before that, I invite you to consider an alternative approach to these challenges, one that incorporate softness. I propose a kinder self-appraisal and perspective; a way to see ourselves and relate to our lives that is gentler than the ways many of us have learned. It is called SOFTT.

What is SOFTT?

SOFTT is the acronym for my step-by-step process to navigate common midlife experiences. It is a deliberate method to slow down, observe our thoughts and emotions, feel the depth and variety of our bodily sensations, and apply tenderness to whatever is on our plates. Through the process, we gradually release the clinging to our thoughts, which enables us to more easily feel our physical bodily sensations. Within this decelerated space, SOFTT also guides us to listen attentively to our inner wisdom. The approach can help us cultivate deeper self-awareness and a greater capacity to both accept and be present to our unfolding lives. It is about riding through life's changing tides, rather than struggling painfully against them.

The acronym SOFTT stands for

1. **S**low down
2. **O**bserve
3. **F**eel
4. **T**enderness
5. **T**une In

Below is a more detailed description of the process.

Step 1: S – Slow Down and Breathe

For most of us, slowing down is not the norm. Rather, we wake up to a flurry of news and emails, multitask throughout the day, and try not to go to sleep before our to-do list is completed. Though this incessant pace can be stressful, we are pleased with our accomplishments and lauded for our achievements and (seeming) efficiency.

Our minds are also constantly on the go. We can jump from thoughts of the past to planning for the future and down unintended rabbit holes, all without pause. "Monkey mind" is a popular term used in Buddhist teachings to capture incessant, non-linear thinking. One study found that people have an average of 6,000 thoughts per day.[7] "Think" about that staggering number for a second!

---

[7]   Tseng, J., Poppenk, J. "Brain Meta-state Transitions Demarcate Thoughts across Task Contexts Exposing the Mental Noise of Trait Neuroticism." *Nature Communications* 11, 3480 (2020.)

Even if this fast physical or mental pace appeals to you, it is less constructive than you realize. When we are in emotionally charged situations (e.g., during or after an argument, amidst a work challenge, or even when we have a hot flash), going 100 mph is almost always ineffective. Hurrying through difficult situations can heighten our emotions, impair our thinking, and blur effective decision-making. It can also induce reactive behaviors, such as saying something in a heated moment which we may later regret, or engaging in frantic efforts to try to "fix" a situation.

It is precisely in these heated moments when we most need and benefit from slowing down, taking a few breaths, and getting some distance from the situation. If you have ever said something like, "Wait, I need a minute to think," that is your mind instinctively telling you to slow down.

To slow down means to dial back the intensity of an action or thought. It is a conscious deceleration. Slowing down is what we do on a treadmill when we need to take a break, or how we drive a car when we approach a turn in the road. In neither situation do we screech to a stop.

I intentionally did not use the word "stop" to capture the first step of the SOFTT process. Stop is more commanding and insensitive; it is not soft. "Stop" can imply that you are doing something wrong, which may automatically invoke a defensive or reactive "No!" Certainly, if you are a passenger in a car and the driver is not slowing down as he approaches a red light, then saying, "Stop!" is appropriate. It necessitates a jolt to wake up in order to prevent possible harm. But most thoughts and behaviors that would benefit from slowing down are not imminently physically dangerous. A softer pause may be more effective.

Here is an example. My friend Jessica called me in a panic after being diagnosed with COVID in 2020. This was before vaccines, when the world was upside down, and when hospitals were reaching capacity. Her symptoms were relatively mild, yet she was terrified considering all of the possibilities that *could* happen. I barely understood what she was saying in her distraught state.

"Jessica," I gently said, "I cannot understand you. Slow down for a minute and take a breath." She paused and I heard her deeply inhale and exhale. "Now, explain to me what's going on." She went on to express her fears, but in a more collected state. The pause and focused breath enabled Jessica to speak, and think, in a more coherent manner and reduced her anxiety and stress.

Benefits of Slowing Down

When we slow down, we can get some space from automatic reactions and gain perspective. Imagine a time when you were disappointed in the outcome of a work or volunteer project that you organized. You may have thought, "I blew it," "I should have done..." or perhaps even, "I'm a terrible leader." That was your inner critic—your internal judge—at play. Our inner critic often resists being told to stop. "But it's true" or "I did blow it!" are examples of resistance.

But if you ask your inner critic to slow down and dial back the criticism, it can be more receptive. This space can offer some emotional relief in the moment and make room for perspective: Did I really blow it or was it more akin to a good rather than great outcome? Am I actually a terrible leader or was this project simply not my best? These are likely more realistic appraisals of the situation.

In addition to helping us pull back from reactive, spiraling thoughts and behaviors, slowing down can bring us clarity. Just this morning, Anna, a regular participant in my weekly meditation group, shared her experience in this realm. She explained that she had been grappling with a situation for weeks, uncertain how to proceed. To her surprise and delight, the answer "appeared" with absolute clarity during her meditation. Anna asked why I thought this happened. "Because you slowed down and gave the issue space from your circular thoughts. You gave it room to percolate in your body, which allowed the answer to come to you in an embodied way," I replied. Though I cannot guarantee that answers will always appear with such ease from slowing down, when we give our issues breathing room, we open ourselves up to the possibility.

A simple, accessible, and effective way to slow down is to take at least three deep, intentional breaths. When we are stressed, our sympathetic nervous system is stimulated, which propels us into the well-known "fight or flight" response. This can cause us to take short, shallow breaths, increase our heart rate, and elevate our blood pressure. When we take slow, full breaths, it helps regulate the automatic physiological response, and activate our parasympathetic, "rest and digest" nervous system. This latter system helps calm our elevated bodily responses which, in turn, can decrease our feelings of anxiety and distress. And it prepares us for Step 2.

Step 2: O – Observe and Release Your Thoughts and Emotions

After you slow down and consciously breathe, the next step is to observe your thoughts and emotions from this quieter physical and mental state. To observe means to take one step back and watch yourself in the situation, as if you are seeing yourself in this moment on a movie screen.

Consider an uncomfortable interaction you had with a colleague or friend. In your mind's eye, picture or imagine watching the scene play out on a movie screen. Take as much time as you need to re-connect with the interaction. Then observe what you, on the screen, are thinking. Your thoughts may be that this person is a jerk, that he has no respect for you, or what you wished you had said at the time.

After you observe a thought, imagine it fading like a cloud in the sky or placing it in a box and gently closing the lid.

Do the same process with your emotions. While watching the imaginary screen, observe if you are mad, resentful, humiliated, insecure, threatened, etc. Notice the array of emotions, some of which may even seem confusing, and then release them.

Be mindful to not restrict, judge, or censor any of your thoughts or emotions, even if they seem contradictory. The encouragement is simply to notice the entirety of your thoughts and emotions, happening right now, for however long it takes. After you observe them, release them.

In the anecdote above, my friend Jessica, in her more collected, slower state, observed her thoughts around the prospect of her COVID symptoms becoming worse, the loss of income if she were unable to work, and concern over who would care for her kids. She observed her emotional reactions of fear, anxiety, and helplessness. This observer mode gave Jessica some perspective on her catastrophic thoughts and subsequent emotions.

Benefits of Observing

Observing not only offers perspective but it also helps us to calm down. "Name it to Tame it" is a phrase coined by Dan Siegel, a psychiatrist and founding co-director of the Mindful Awareness Research Center at UCLA. The phrase refers to the relief we can experience after we identify an emotion by name. In other words, when we observe (i.e., name) that we feel angry, hurt, or embarrassed, it can reduce the intensity and impact of the emotion. Siegel further states that when we consciously name an emotion, it initiates a physical response: "It signals the brain to send soothing neurotransmitters to our amygdala, which calms our bodies and minds, and helps us feel more in control."[8] When we observe during SOFTT, we incorporate this practice of noticing the content of our thoughts and our emotions, which can lessen their power over us.

Refrain from Engaging, Analyzing, and Judging

Observing is not an analytical step; it is watching yourself from the sidelines. As you begin this step, you may be tempted to have an inner dialogue about a thought or emotion. For example, in the scene above, you may start to consider other examples of your colleague or friend acting like a jerk. Or, you may observe that you are sad, which may propel you to question why you are sad because mad seems more fitting to the scenario. If you engage in these analytical considerations, you are no longer in an observation mode. Instead, you have begun to join, and even fuel, the thought.

When observing, you need not understand why you think or feel a certain way. There is dedicated time and space for that in the last step of the process, at which time inquiring will be more effective. Furthermore, insights around your thoughts and emotions may naturally arise after you allow yourself time to thoroughly observe them.

Another tendency when we are in observation mode is to question whether our thoughts are accurate, something we seldom consider unless we have some distance from them. Instead, we tend to assume our thoughts are true simply because we think them. With the space that comes with observing, we may now question their accuracy. Some thoughts may be true, but it's likely that more are not. It is important to explore the truthfulness of our thoughts, but not when we are observing them. We can revisit these inquiries when we are further along in the SOFTT process.

---

[8] mindfulness.com/mindful-living/name-it-to-tame-it.

These analytical questions around our thoughts and emotions are actually a positive sign; they demonstrate that we have begun to separate a bit from them. In other words, the distance from observing enables us to loosen our grip on them.

Another important aspect within this observational step is to refrain from judging our thoughts and emotions. This is an integral part of most mindfulness practices. In fact, Jon Kabat-Zinn, a renowned mindfulness expert and founder of the popular Mindfulness Based Stress Reduction program, defines mindfulness as "awareness that arises through paying attention, on purpose, in the present moment, non-judgmentally."[9]

For many, the non-judgmental aspect of awareness is a particular challenge, since it is a departure from how we commonly interact with uncomfortable thoughts and emotions. "That's a terrible thought" or "I shouldn't feel resentful" are examples of judging or criticizing what is naturally coming up for us. Judgment not only takes us away from observing, it adds another layer of suffering. You have that thought and you feel resentful. Period.

To observe is to allow oneself to see everything that arises, even if we do not like what we think or feel. The thoughts and feelings are still there. They are simply cognitions and emotions related to our present state. When we refrain from judgment, we can see them more clearly, more truthfully.

What if observing is difficult?

Sometimes it can be difficult to decipher specific thoughts or emotions, especially in times of distress. They may appear as a confusing muddle of many thoughts and feelings that are hard to de-tangle. If

[9]   https://www.mindful.org/jon-kabat-zinn-defining-mindfulness

you cannot identify them, that is okay. Just accept that they exist, observe the whole mess of thoughts and feelings, and let them go.

An alternative approach, for when you cannot easily parse your thoughts and emotions, is to switch to a passive observer mode. As you picture yourself on the movie screen, try using a third-party prefix such as "She thinks…" or "She feels..." This approach automatically places you outside of yourself and into observer mode. For example, Jessica, in referring to herself, could have said, "Jessica thinks she may get really sick," or "Jessica feels scared and helpless."

Remember, the thoughts and emotions, in and of themselves, are not necessarily the problem. The challenge is when we get hijacked by their force, and spiral into a tornado of thoughts and emotions, without breathing room or perspective. As Donna Henes beautifully writes in *The Queen of Myself*, "Once we have connected with our emotions…we can accept them as our teachers, bow to their great lessons, embrace them with love, and then release them into the night."[10]

In sum, observe and allow any and all thoughts and emotions that are present to arise and then release them. Do your best to give them their freedom to be noticed, without censor, judgment, or engagement. Allow them to flow and release like untethered tears. You may even experience relief in the process, in the same way many of us feel better after a good cry.

Then you're ready for Step 3.

Step 3: F – Feel Your Bodily Sensations

Step 3 moves us from a place of objective and dispassionate observation to one of engaged awareness of the physical sensations in our bodies. It is common, when in emotionally overwhelming states, to

---

[10]   Henes, D. (2004). *The Queen of My Self: Stepping into Sovereignty in Midlife*. Monarch Press, p. 129.

become disconnected from our bodies, and mostly associate with our thoughts. This step reconnects us with our physicality. We shift, for example, from being an observer of our fearful thoughts on the movie screen, to stepping into the scene and feeling our array of physical sensations associated with fear.

Step 3, like Step 2 before, is best served with a measure of courage and self-respect: courage to intentionally drop into whatever physical sensations are present (e.g., flurries in your belly, tightness in your jaws, etc.) and self-respect to honor yourself sufficiently in order to enter the movie screen and really own what is alive for you in the moment.

When I am anxious, my skin gets clammy, my heart beats faster, and I get knots in my belly. Paradoxically, when I am excited, I experience similar bodily sensations. When I am sad, my body is heavy and my jaws ache. When I am angry, my neck and shoulders tighten. Being present to these sensations connects me with what is actually happening viscerally.

After Jessica aired her concerns related to her COVID diagnosis, I guided her to tune in to her body—to turn her attention to the sensations in her muscles, skin, and organs. She described feeling huge waves in her belly and tightness in her shoulders, both of which she was unaware of when lost in her panic over contagiousness, the necessity to quarantine, and the number of lives lost to COVID. She also described a heaviness, as if she could not move. I encouraged her to experience these sensations, without judgment, in order to reconnect with her body. With this as her focus, she became less caught up in her future-oriented thoughts.

Some people resist feeling their bodily sensations. They may not want to experience discomfort or may fear that it will make the experience worse. Bringing awareness to our physical sensations does not typically amplify them. In fact, sometimes they lessen in intensity. According to Caroline Welch, author of *The Gift of Presence,* "Aversion (to unpleasant experiences) makes them worse; the more we...try to push them away, the more we become exhausted and generate even more unpleasant feelings."[11]

Try it for a minute and see what happens. If it becomes too overwhelming, pause and take a few deep breaths or park this step until you are less physically overloaded.

Then we move on to Step 4.

Step 4: T – Apply Tenderness

This step of the SOFTT process is all about being tender toward ourselves. Here is where we intentionally treat ourselves with kindness and compassion; we are as gentle with ourselves as we would be with our best friend or a child who is suffering.

A simple and effective approach to tenderness is to acknowledge our situation by using words such as "This is hard," or "This hurts." These tender words help us to connect with and appreciate the challenge of the moment, rather than get lost in details or self-pity. When we add a gentle physical touch, such as placing our hand on our heart as we say the words, it helps solidify the intention.

Think of a time when you confided in a friend about something difficult. What did she say to you that was soothing or comforting? If your confidant responded with, "Well, at least such and such didn't happen," or "I'm sure it wasn't that bad," those comments, even if well-intended, probably did not alleviate your pain. In fact, they may have caused you to feel dismissed, minimized, or unheard.

In contrast, if the response was more along the lines of, "Wow, that's a lot," or "That sounds really difficult," you most likely

---

[11] Welch, C. *The Gift of Presence: A Mindfulness Guide for Women*, Tarcher-Perigee, 2021. pp 12-13.

experienced some softening around the challenge as a result of being heard and seen. Your friend appreciated your pain. Just as we feel soothed when a friend acknowledges our pain, we can also feel soothed when we offer this verbal tenderness to ourselves.

Your friend may have reached out to touch you in a show of support, and to affirm your pain. Many of us, especially women, instinctively use physical connection to acknowledge another's suffering—we may offer a hug, a light touch, or wrap our arm around their shoulder. These gestures do not require words. The physical connection speaks volumes.

This same tactile gesture, when applied to ourselves, is active self-compassion. I automatically put my hand on my heart when I'm in need of soothing self-compassion. And when I touch my heart and then tell myself, "This is hard," it is doubly helpful.

In my call with Jessica, I validated her concerns by commenting, "This sounds rough." "Yeah, it is," she replied. She stayed with that sentiment, rather than return to her specific COVID fears. "I can't hug you, so give yourself a reassuring hug from me, will you?" I asked. "Thanks, will do," she said, her voice softer, slower, and lower than it was at the beginning of our conversation.

When we apply tenderness to ourselves, it is important to do so consciously, with intention, and to allow the words and gestures to fully wash over us. Methodically reciting them is less effective. Choose words that work for you, and that are true in the moment, and allow their truth to root in your body. I promise that you will experience the shift.

Tenderness can be used at any point or points in the SOFTT process but I believe it is most effective in the fourth step. As I developed and applied SOFTT, I found that it could be difficult to apply tenderness right out of the gate, especially if the situation is emotionally intense. I was sometimes not ready; I needed the space and pause of Step 1.

I also found that when I applied tenderness too early, it muted the fullness of the previous steps; it impeded me from the ability to observe my full range of thoughts and emotions and to experience the array of associated sensations in my body.

Tenderness, while sounding simple and, perhaps to some, even silly, is a critical step. I never cease to be awed by the power of a few comforting words and a gentle physical gesture. I encourage you to try it, even if it feels unnatural or weird. There is literally no scenario in which self-compassion is not helpful—especially when we think we do not need or deserve it.

And now, we turn to the last step.

Step 5: T – Tune In to Your Inner Wisdom

Jon Kabat-Zinn sometimes adds the following words to his definition of mindfulness: "...nonjudgmental awareness *in the service of self-understanding and wisdom.*"[12] His expansion of his definition implies that greater awareness heightens our ability to know ourselves and gain wisdom.

I offer to you that nonjudgmental awareness also aids in accessing wisdom that already resides within us; it sets the stage for us to tap into our existing well of inner wisdom.

Though our inner wisdom is always there, we sometimes forget it, especially when in the midst of a struggle. Our minds can get fuzzy and we can lose access to our life's lessons. This is exemplified when we say things such as "When am I going to learn?" "I keep forgetting _____," or "Why did I say yes? I should have known better." This wisdom is not gone; it is earned and stored in our body and mind. It is simply that when our thinking gets cloudy, we lose connection

---

[12]   https://www.mindful.org/jon-kabat-zinn-defining-mindfulness.

to our wisdom, and succumb to our long-standing conditioning to look outside ourselves for answers and counsel.

Often, within the slower, quieter state that can arise from Steps 1 through 4, we regain the access and ability to uncover, and recover, the treasure trove of lessons, truths, experiences, and intuition that live inside of us. This wisdom can help us to skillfully address our present situation, understand our reactions, and find clarity and direction.

We can tune in to our wisdom by asking ourselves specific questions. For example:

* Are my beliefs true? Was he really a jerk or am I being defensive?

* What has helped me during past difficult times? (Answers such as "I usually feel better when I talk with a friend or spend some time in nature" can surface.)

* What lessons can I take from this experience? (Perhaps your inner wisdom reminds you to listen to your instincts or to say no, despite pressure to say yes.)

* What advice would I give my best friend if she were experiencing this? (Would you tell her not to be so hard on herself or that she is not giving herself enough credit?)

* What resources or help do I need? Do I need information, alone time, professional help, etc.?

* What do I need to remember? (Perhaps "This too shall pass," or "I've made it through difficult times before" ring true for you.)

* Is there anything I actually can and need to "do"? Or is the wisdom, "It is what it is," more fitting? (Helplessness is an enormously challenging feeling. But sometimes, the wisdom is that there is simply nothing you can do other than to tenderly experience and own your sense of helplessness.)

SOFTT aids us to access answers like these. We can explore the accuracy of our beliefs, recall past difficulties we endured, and remember how valuable it can be to take a solo walk, or have an empathic sounding board, such as that provided by a friend or therapist. We can then use this wisdom as a bright inner compass to illuminate our path.

Consider these examples:

When Jessica tuned in to her inner wisdom, she realized the catastrophic nature of her thoughts. Even if her symptoms worsened, she would likely not warrant hospitalization and, if so, she had friends who would look after her kids. She acknowledged that calling me had helped and that her next call would be to her doctor for valid medical input.

Petra was often anxious when her twenty-three-year-old daughter was traveling solo overseas. She frequently got lost in "what if" thoughts and was nervous whenever her daughter did not quickly respond to texts. Using SOFTT, Petra explored some of her catastrophic thoughts: What if she gets sick? What if she puts herself in a dangerous situation? What if…? Petra then "remembered" that her daughter is very responsible, that she raised her to be independent, and that Petra herself seldom checked in with her own parents when she traveled during her twenties. Her daughter was likely doing the same thing Petra did at twenty-three, reveling in her new adventure and having fun. Petra relaxed her automatic "mom thoughts" and instead, mentally wished her daughter fun and safety. Her inner wisdom guided her to ask her daughter to please text her every three days, with a simple "All is good." Her daughter agreed to Petra's easy request.

How we "remember" our inner wisdom is as varied as we are; sometimes it just shows up when we give our incessant thoughts a break. Petra's did when she paused, and Anna from my meditation group found her inner wisdom during a meditation practice. Other times, we can "remember" by journaling or even reading past journals.

Two months after my brother Eddie died, which was nine months after my father passed, I was in one of the most difficult chapters of my life. I was devastated and lost. I had consulted with a few therapists though had not yet connected with the one who ultimately became instrumental in my healing. I was functioning but that was about it. I felt literally broken and my tears seemed like they would never end. That same month my youngest daughter, then a high school senior, was visiting universities to make her final decision on where to attend. My husband, daughter, and I were scheduled to fly to Berkeley for a university tour.

During a morning meditation a few days before our trip, I had the epiphany (i.e., inner wisdom) that I needed to get away for a "healing journey." I had no idea what that journey would entail but I knew it was necessary. When I told this to my husband, he wholeheartedly agreed. "Take some time, do what you need to do to soothe your soul," was my amazing husband's reply.

So, rather than fly, my husband, daughter, and I drove up to Berkeley to tour the school together. Two days later, I dropped them off at the airport to return to San Diego, while I headed north in our car to begin my "healing journey." I tearfully said goodbye, uncertain where this journey would take me. My sweet daughter reminded me that I could come home whenever I wanted and my husband gave me a tight, reassuring hug. Off I went, loaded with my meditation cushion, journal, books, and a list of podcasts.

My five-day healing journey, though occasionally challenging, was magical and rich with gifts I gratefully received. One morning while journaling, I had a profound insight related to my grief over Eddie. I realized that I had ambivalence to saying farewell to those deep, sorrowful tears because it was in those moments of intense sadness that I felt closest to Eddie. And with that awareness, I saw the need in myself to develop other joyful ways to connect with him. That was a powerful epiphany. Listening to my wisdom to take time and space to heal was spot-on.

Christiane Northrup, MD, author of several books, including the New York Times Bestseller, *The Wisdom of Menopause*, offered the following advice: "Hold the intention to connect with your inner wisdom. Be open to what might arise."[13] I would add, ask for it, listen to it, and use it as your inner and outer compass.

When to Use SOFTT

Jessica's COVID situation was one illustration of SOFTT's value in a moment of panic, but its use is not limited to extreme situations. It can be helpful anytime and anywhere, but especially when we find ourselves spinning in thoughts or emotions, needing to change gears, or would benefit from a reset. You can use SOFTT when you are anxious, confused, or in a grumpy mood. You can use SOFTT when you spill coffee on your white pants, or before and after a difficult interaction. You can use SOFTT between clients or meetings; when your kids, parents, colleagues, or partner trigger you; or when you discover your passport has expired on the eve of a long-awaited trip to Europe (my actual freak-out a few years back). SOFTT can help you celebrate unexpected good news and digest bad news, revel for a moment in how you feel in a cool outfit or when you are frustrated that the outfit is too tight. You can pause and apply tenderness to literally any situation.

---

[13]   Northrup, C. *The Wisdom of Menopause: Creating Physical and Emotional Health During the Change*, Bantam Dell, 2001

The Bottom Line

To embrace the middle is to invite softness into our lives. It is a path to self-awareness that invokes and applies presence, compassion, and wisdom to the difficult and joyful passages that are inherent in midlife. The SOFTT step-by-step process guides us to slow down and breathe, observe our thoughts and emotions, fully experience our bodily sensations, apply tenderness, and tune in to our inner wisdom.

When we pause and observe, it can provide some distance from our spinning thoughts and increase our awareness of our inner landscape. When we feel our physical sensations, it reconnects us with our bodies and what is happening within us on a visceral level. When we apply tenderness, it softens our hearts and minds and affords us the broader perspective of "this is difficult." And sometimes, space and tenderness can open the pathways to remember and uncover our deep-seated wisdom. The process is a courageous, intimate exploration of ourselves in the moment, which not only softens the path, but can lead to clarity, healing, and direction.

Remember that softness and SOFTT are a journey, not a destination. I encourage you to embark on the SOFTT process with curiosity and an open heart. Be patient and gentle with yourself, and appreciate that cultivating presence and compassion take time and effort.

In Part 2, I share the highest-ranking challenges and gifts of midlife, according to the hundreds of women who answered the survey and illustrate how to apply SOFTT, using examples for both challenges and gifts. I regularly use SOFTT in my own life, with my individual clients, and in my workshops. Almost universally, women have found it to be a valuable, awakening endeavor. My hope is that you, too, will find it to be both enlightening and beneficial, not only in helping you navigate your midlife's challenges, but also in celebrating your experience-earned growth and achievements.

Part 2

What to Embrace

CHAPTER 5

MIDLIFE CHALLENGES

"It is your reaction to adversity, not adversity itself, that determines how your life's story will develop.'

—Dieter F. Uchtdorf

In spring of 2023, I surprised myself by going to see the much-hyped movie, *Barbie*. I went with nine girlfriends, all dressed in pink, and we even posed for a group selfie in front of the theater marquee. I was reluctant to go since Barbie represents an ageless, stereotypical standard of beauty that is unattainable for most, and unsustainable for all. Why would I support a movie that does not speak to beauty in all forms, including the kind that comes with age? I obviously knew little of Ruth Handler's laudable intention to create dolls that empower girls (there were no doll scientists when I played with them way back when) nor that some of my criticisms mentioned above would be addressed head-on in the movie.

I was delightfully surprised. The movie was funny, at times deep, and a powerful testament to the experience of being a woman in a patriarchal society. My group of ten ranged in age from forty-two to seventy-nine and, despite our age gamut, we all related to at least one aspect of the female reality. Whether it was our inability to see our aging beauty, our alienation from our power, or being dismissed by men, the themes struck close to home.

If you have not seen the movie, Barbie's mornings in "Barbie Land" are comical. She wakes up looking gorgeous, with a huge smile on her face. She brushes her straight white teeth, puts on an adorable outfit, and joyfully eats her pretend breakfast. Barbie then heads to work (i.e., the beach) in her pink convertible, while waving to her many adoring male and female friends.

Over post-movie margaritas (which helped wash down the greasy popcorn), I asked my friends what would make for a perfect morning in a utopian "Midlife Land." Here is what we came up with:

> 7:00 – Wake up rested after a solid eight hours of sleep. (I personally could stop there and would be thrilled.)
> 7:10 – Get out of bed without anything creaking or hurting.
> 7:20 – Look in the mirror and love what we see, regardless of any wrinkles, dark circles, or sagging.
> 7:30 – Complete a hard workout without hurting ourselves.
> 8:15 – Check our phones to find a text from our kids, telling us how much they love and appreciate us.
> 8:20 – Ditto from our parents/parents-in-law, with the added note that they feel great today.
> 8:25 – Find a cute outfit in record time, which to our surprise, fits loosely.
> 8:30 – Eat a delicious leisurely breakfast, prepared by anyone but ourselves, followed by an effortless bowel movement.
> 8:50 – Head to a job we love, and where we are seen and appreciated for our experience and competence.

We were laughing so hard, we never came up with any activities past nine a.m. Jokes aside, our dream morning touched on a number of very real midlife themes: elusive sleep, body aches and vulnerabilities, weight gain, children and parent worries, job burnout, and our experience of invisibility. When we were goofing around and creating our perfect morning, we did not need to name our challenges; they were obvious. We laughed in agreement, or perhaps commiseration, at each one.

My question about the perfect morning illuminated my pursuit to understand and reveal women's midlife reality. I was curious to know which specific concerns weigh on us most heavily. And, I was eager to unpack the varied ways these challenges impact our lives and those around us.

In the 2020 survey, I inquired about specific midlife struggles I believed to be most prevalent, based on my personal journey and those of my friends and clients. These included several that my friends and I jokingly highlighted years later in our midlife utopian morning. In the follow-up interviews, with a subset of survey participants, we explored their answers in more depth. The interviews were also an opportunity for women to discuss challenges that were not included in the survey categories.

Below is the exact wording and order of the survey questions that addressed midlife challenges. Before you read the results, I invite you to first answer the questions yourself using the instructions below.

Directions: Rate each of the following categories on the following four-point scale: (1) not at all concerned, (2) mildly concerned, (3) somewhat concerned, or (4) very concerned. If the category is not applicable to your life, just skip it. When you're done, identify your highest scoring (i.e., most concerning) categories and write them in the space below.

"Thinking about the past few years (i.e., pre-COVID), how much do these midlife issues concern you as compared to your twenties and thirties?"

	Category	Your Ranking*
1	Health and Body Decline	
2	Well-Being of Kids	
3	Enough Money (e.g., retirement, kids' college, support to others, etc.)	
4	Caregiver Responsibilities (e.g., parents, in-laws, grown children, etc.)	
5	Existential Questions of Value, Worth, Direction, Life, etc.	
6	Physical Appearance Changes	
7	Relationships (e.g., marital, friends, colleagues, etc.)	
8	Hormonal Changes/Imbalances	
9	Work/Career Dissatisfaction	
10	Other (describe)	
	Two additional areas not included in the written survey which came up frequently in the interviews:	
11	Death and Loss	
12	Middle Ageism (i.e., stereotypes, ageism, invisibility)	

*Rank Degree of concern as 1 (not at all), 2 (mildly), 3 (somewhat) or 4 (very concerning)

Your highest-scoring concerns:

1. _____

2. _____

3. _____

The data revealed that, collectively, our top "very concerning" midlife issues are:

1. Health and Body Decline
2. Death and Loss
3. Kids, Caregiving, and Cash

In looking at the top three concerns, challenges in any one of these areas can be life changing. And when we face two, three, or four concurrently, which *is* the common midlife reality, we can become overwhelmed.

I was equally surprised by two issues that did *not* rank toward the top of the "very concerning" category: hormonal fluctuations and physical appearance issues. These relatively lower rankings do not imply that hormonal fluctuations, our changing appearance, and shifting relationships (another relatively low-scoring area) are not a big deal. They absolutely are. And for some of us, they are monumental. Ask anyone dealing with brain fog that impacts their capacity to work, excess weight they cannot shed regardless of what they do, or a divorce, and they will educate you on how colossal these challenges can be. *Rather, the results shed light on the less discussed but highly significant co-occurring difficulties of the middle decades.*

Furthermore, as I dove deeper and parsed the statistics and interviews, I realized that some of the physical challenges of hormonal fluctuations are likely represented in the "health and bodily decline" category. I address this issue at length further in this chapter and in Appendix 2.

Let's unpack these categories and take a peek at some of the individual stories behind the answers.

Health and Body Decline

Health and body decline is overarchingly the greatest midlife challenge. Even if we do not mentally connect with our age, our bodies are undeniably older and more vulnerable. We anxiously await our mammogram results, can seldom read small print, and answer "what?" with increasing frequency. Sound sleep is elusive for most and our aches and pains do not seem to leave. They just relocate. As one interviewee said, "I can't believe it. I actually make noises when I stand up."

These are the most common physical challenges women talked about in the interviews:

* Fatigue and Less Energy
* Aches and Pains (including our joints and knees)
* Weight Gain
* Declining Vision
* Impaired Sleep
* Sexual Issues
* Brain Fog/Forgetfulness

Some of these physical changes are expected in midlife. However, many of us also experience the onset of some entirely unexpected physical challenges. I was never forewarned that midlife can include memory challenges and anxiety, two issues commonly associated with perimenopause and menopause. When I talked with my girlfriends, I was relieved that they too experienced them. But until I talked with them, I heard nothing but crickets in terms of what to expect in this phase of life.

We also tend to get physically hurt more easily (that little slip we would have laughed off in our younger years can now send us hobbling to the chiropractor) and are slower to recover from injuries and illnesses. We are more concerned that little things might be big things and that big things might turn into bigger things. More than one woman bemoaned the inability to have a couple extra cocktails without feeling the effects for much of the next day. I can sadly relate.

This is also the time in our lives when some of us, myself included, have to start taking medications for health purposes. That is a hard pill to swallow—literally; We cannot be *that* old. I had to start taking cholesterol medication at age fifty-six. No matter how much I exercise and how well I eat (or am willing to eat), genetics prevail. It is always unsettling when I read the small print on my statin bottle: "This pill is intended to help prevent strokes and heart attacks." Ouch! My brain interprets that as me being old and physically vulnerable. Similarly, how about when we go to medical appointments and have to rattle off our growing list of medications and supplements? It can be disconcerting when our bodies increasingly need these aids to function optimally and yet I am immensely grateful that they exist.

What was also interesting in regard to our physicality is the disconnect between what we want to do physically (and sometimes think we can) and what our bodies can actually still do. This is especially true for women who were always physically active. We think we can still ski black (i.e., advanced) slopes—and hooray for you if you can—and are humbled when we have to stop to catch our breath a few times or feel it in our knees for several days afterward. Our brains say yes, while our bodies say, "Maybe not."

As one interviewee said, "I don't want to surrender to the physical part of aging." I get it. It is a bummer when our bodies do not fully cooperate with our desires.

Even more challenging, by midlife, some of us have had or currently have serious health challenges. This was the case for several women in the study, with cancer being the most prevalent disease.

And when this happens, we are not only physically challenged by the symptoms and treatments but also by collateral worries: Will there be enough money, especially if I cannot work? Who will care for my kids or parents if I am unable? And ultimately, will I survive? These are serious, scary, and very real considerations.

If we are fortunate to have not faced a major health challenge, many of us have growing fears of getting diagnosed with one, especially those who are genetically predisposed to specific diseases. This fear is rational. We have arrived at the age where we have friends and family who have battled and sometimes died from serious diseases. And for some of the women I interviewed, they were catching up to the age when their parents had passed and wondered whether their lifespans would exceed their parents.

I can think of at least seven close friends who have had breast cancer, another one who is in treatment for thyroid cancer, and a brother who had a major heart attack at only fifty-nine. And, in the past few years, I have lost another brother to heart disease, a first cousin to leukemia, a very close friend to lung cancer, and another dear friend to breast cancer. They were all in their mid-fifties to early sixties and in seemingly good health. I would wager most of you have also experienced losses of relatively young friends and family members.

And this brings us to our next category: Death and Loss.

Death and Loss

Midlife is awash with big losses and smaller, yet still impactful losses. The big ones are of course the deaths of our loved ones—our parents, partners, siblings, other relatives, friends, and even societal heroes and icons. Those losses are deep and life changing. And sometimes, we lose these people long before they die. When I expressed my condolences to a friend after her mother passed, she replied, "I lost her ten years ago to dementia and have been grieving ever since. It was just her body that was left." In circumstances like these, death can be a sad relief.

Death leaves voids that are simply impossible to fill. The pain, which at times can seem insurmountable, is raw and deep. As one woman said, "I am pained by not having my parents' presence on earth. It physically hurts." "I still can't fathom life without my mom. She was my best friend and the best grandmother," said another.

The death of a parent, spouse, or even more tragically a child, challenges and changes us like nothing else. And we face our own mortality in a very real way. Whether it is losing people, or losing who they once were as they decline, it is an unparalleled challenge that brings unparalleled pain.

Ripple Effects of Death

In addition to the direct emotional pain, death appears to have the widest ripple effect of all of the midlife challenges. Octavia worked closely with her father in a business he co-owned with a partner. When her father died, her position in the company died alongside him. The business partner was not especially fond of Octavia despite (or perhaps because) of her intimate knowledge of the company. Although she was an indisputable asset to the business, she has already been demoted and fears that she will ultimately be fired now that her father is gone. This is a huge double loss for Octavia.

For me, losing my parents was also losing my roots. For the first time, my birthplace, New Orleans, no longer felt like home. Even though I had not lived there for nearly forty years, when my parents were alive it was still home, and the house I grew up in was home base. But with their deaths, all of that changed.

Parents are also frequently the glue that holds families together. Siblings who are caught in conflict with one another sometimes rally together when it comes to their parents. They may suspend their differences and be cordial at milestone celebrations and funerals. But what happens to those relationships when the glue is gone? I am in that situation now. With both parents and our sibling leader deceased, and some long-standing, deep-seated sibling conflicts, our party of four (three years ago, we were a party of seven) is figuring out how to navigate family-of-origin life issues without our glue. It is a painful and difficult work in progress. For some of the women I interviewed, their sibling relationships did not heal and each went their separate way.

Other "Deaths"

In addition to literal deaths, we experience other losses in midlife, which get downplayed in terms of their relative significance. Our visibility, our wrinkle-free skin, and our ability to bear children, to name a few. Though these losses may not be as deep or sorrowful as the deaths of dear ones, they are still losses and represent a different kind of death.

One of mine was the necessity to stop jogging, after forty years, as a result of too much wear and tear and injury to my knees. I still remember the moment the doctor called with my MRI results. I was in my car in a Bed Bath & Beyond parking lot. "I'm amazed that you've been running this long without severe pain," he said. "You are bone-on-bone in multiple areas and have a torn meniscus. The only thing that can help is a knee replacement but you're too young for that. You'd probably outlive it and need another one. I suggest you hang up your running shoes, take up swimming, and we can talk about a knee replacement down the road."

I felt like I was punched in the stomach. I was stunned and devastated. Stop running? I'm a runner. It's part of my identity. I had been jogging since age twelve. I had just run my twentieth half marathon a few months before. I had always assumed I would be one of those women who still ran 10ks into her seventies. I also assumed I would always be able to hike challenging trails, and meditate in half lotus, but those activities were also impacted by my aging knees.

We have all "lost" something or someone by the time we reach the middle decades. But just as with our physical decline, it is ultimately easier to accept and embrace the losses, with presence and compassion, than it is to deny, ignore, or resent these growing realities.

Caregiving, Kids, and Cash

Because of gains in life expectancy, more and more middle-aged adults are taking on caregiver roles for their parents, including financial aspects, while still having to juggle work and raise children. My research supports this reality. Taking care of our elders and concerns over the well-being of our kids were neck and neck as our next biggest concerns after health and loss, with financial worries close behind. Collectively, these findings shine a bright light on the intense challenges of the "sandwich generation" crunch: simultaneously caring for the generations above and below us.

The implications of this crunch are big. A national survey of caregivers over the age of fifty found that "among those who had worked while caregiving, two-thirds had made some adjustments to their employment because of their caregiving responsibilities, such as taking time off, taking a leave of absence, cutting back work hours, or turning down a promotion. One in ten caregivers quit a job or took early retirement."[14] Given that women are more likely than men to be the familial caregivers, these findings disproportionately affect us.

---

[14] National Alliance for Caregiving (NAC) and AARP. *Caregiving in the U.S.* Bethesda, MD: NAC, and Washington, DC: AARP, November 2009.

We will explore each of the three categories (caregiving, kids, and cash) separately, with the appreciation that for many, they occur simultaneously. This may partly explain why they were tied in the ranking of midlife concerns.

Caregiving

Caregiving is a challenge that can impact us on many levels: practical, emotional, physical, and, for many, financial. The psychological impact alone, of shifting from being cared for by our parents to caring for them, can be huge.

Our parents are living longer, some of their conditions necessitate significant assistance, and many did not invest in long-term care insurance policies. This means it often falls on the offspring to supplement their living and medical expenses. This is an aspect of midlife that many of us, myself included, did not consider in decades prior or prepare for financially.

In addition to financial considerations, there are the many unknowns of health outcomes. What if a parent gets dementia? What if one or both become physically disabled? What if the more independent parent passes first? What if we are not able to care for them?

Just considering the various scenarios is stressful, worrisome, and emotionally trying. I know firsthand because I'm currently grappling with these issues and they weigh on me heavily. Most of us would like to help our elders, at least to a degree, yet we cannot always be that resource, even if it is our heart's desire. These are difficult and layered situations and decisions.

Caretaking is a labor of love. It requires physical and emotional energy, patience, and dedicated time, which is time away from other activities and people. Sarai shared her struggle with this issue. She and her mother were always very close and she had planned to care for her when she got older. Yet, the more her mother declined and the greater her needs, the more it physically and emotionally taxed Sarai. "I would leave her house and cry all the way home. She was this feeble little thing. It broke my heart to see her like that and I had less and less to give to my husband and kids." Sarai eventually decided to dip into her retirement funds to hire a nurse because the emotional cost of continuing to be her mother's caretaker was too high.

Disagreements can also arise among family members with regards to caretaking, medical decisions, and uneven distribution of responsibilities. Often, the offspring who live closest to the parents carry the extra burden. This can complicate decision-making and even inheritance allocation after a parent passes.

The following comment from an anonymous survey taker illustrates how often women become the caretakers, and the cost of that role. "I already took care of both sets of parents till death. My concerns now are for my children and grandchild facing difficult times. My worst worry is taking care of my husband, who is fighting a serious form of cancer—how difficult will this be for him, and if I will be able to give him the care he will need. I've spent over nineteen years caring for others; it's a stressful job. It's one I am more than willing to do, but it is wearing. It takes a toll mentally and physically. This is my main worry." This amazing woman's remarks illustrate the real bind some women face—a desire to caretake but the inability to know for certain if we have the resources, ability, or energy for the job.

There is no absolute right or wrong way when it comes to caretaking. Each situation is unique: the circumstances, resources, and needs of the dependent, our relationship with those in need, and our own emotional, practical, and financial circumstances. It requires many heartfelt, honest conversations, and immense compassion for everyone involved.

Kids

Midlife With Children

For those women with children, the well-being of their kids continues to be a primary concern in midlife. Even if our offspring are adults and no longer live with us, their health and happiness remain foremost in our thoughts. As our kids age alongside us, our concerns shift from worries over their grades and moods, to concerns regarding their safety, choices, and futures.

One mother shared that she easily accepted her daughter being transgender but was worried with how she would be treated in society. What would happen when she left the safety of the cocoon? Another interviewee had to make a significant family decision upon learning her daughter is lesbian. They were long-term members of a church which, on ideological grounds, would never accept her daughter's sexuality. How could she continue to align with an organized religion that rejected her daughter's sexual orientation? She could not. As a result, the entire family left the church. But this loving mom is concerned about other hurdles her daughter may face independently.

Women from several different countries with adult children in the armed forces voiced fear for their children's physical safety. A friend in San Diego has a son in the army. She speaks with him on a monthly basis and sees him only once or twice per year. He is eighteen. Another interviewee has three kids in the Israeli army. Her youngest, at eighteen, just started mandatory service. The middle one is an officer and her oldest in the reserves. Worrying is a major part of her day. Though her son is not in the service, Valerie, who is African American, shared her experiences of racism and her ongoing fear for her son's safety.

A few moms shared their difficult challenge of having kids with mental illnesses or substance abuse issues. These moms support their adult kids and accept that they can only do so much. "I will never stop loving my son but he ultimately has his own journey," said one.

Midlife Without Children

On the other side of the spectrum, several women shared their varied experience of getting older without kids. Estimates are that twenty percent of women do not have biological children, by either choice or circumstance.

Some of the women I interviewed, who chose to not have children, described their absence as liberating. "I knew I did not have the emotional bandwidth and have always been content with my decision," said Tori. "I listen to my friends talk about their kids' struggles and feel for them, but am secretly relieved that's not on my plate," remarked Sylvia. "I get all the joy I need from my nieces and nephews, without the hard parts," remarked another.

Other women expressed frustration that people judge them, even in midlife, for choosing to not have children. "I always knew I did not want kids yet even in my fifties, people still asked me why. It's frustrating," Melody shared. "I don't fit the mold," said Sandy. "I don't have kids, I never married, and my career as a clairvoyant is untraditional. I feel like most people don't know how to relate to me." Christina, age sixty-two, said that she has always felt ashamed for not desiring children even though she unequivocally "did not want the emotional strain" of parenting.

Most of the women I interviewed, who wanted but were unable to have children, had arrived at a necessary acceptance of the situation. Their infertility chapters, now over, were physically and emotionally brutal. What remains for some, however, is the pity they sometimes feel from others. "IVF was hard enough. It literally bankrupted us and almost cost our marriage as well. But people feeling sorry for you makes it way worse. I always wanted kids but was never able. I wished people would realize how awful it feels to be pitied. Plus, it brings back that yearning and sorrow all over again," said Pauline.

A few interviewees mentioned specific concerns relative to the absence of children. The first worry was who would look after them should they need assistance as they age. Though certainly not all children rise to this task, offspring are commonly expected to eventually care for their parents. Few of us have friends or other relatives who would be able or willing to take on this role.

The second concern voiced by women without children relates to thoughts of their legacy in the absence of kids. Tori said, "Maybe I'm unrealistic but when you die and have kids, at least your name and memories of you live on through them and their kids. But when you don't, it's over when you are over. That makes me sad and a little freaked out."

Empty Nests

I could not conclude a section on the role of children in midlife without addressing the "empty nest." Many of us were conditioned to believe that we would be devastated when our kids moved out of our homes. My visual, likely inspired from the media, was a depressed mom, sitting on the bed in her child's vacant bedroom, staring into space, while holding a stuffed animal. And, true to this image, several women in the study were deeply shaken when their kids left home. They discussed not only missing their kids' presence and the unsettling quiet, but also the loss of identity left by the mothering void and unaccustomed free time. This was especially true for moms who chose to stay at home and raise their kids. Some had not considered how they would spend their extra time after decades of tending to the needs of their offspring.

On the contrary, and less openly discussed, are the many other women who eagerly anticipate the freedom that can come with an empty nest. They love their kids *and* are ready to have their own needs and desires front and center. "It's awesome!" said one interviewee. "We love it!" chimed another. My husband and I both cried when our daughters left home. I still get teary-eyed when they return to school after breaks, and it's even harder with our oldest daughter visiting less frequently now that she lives in Europe. And, I love our quieter space, my extra time, and not lying in bed half-asleep until my daughters, regardless of their age, get home safely at night.

Cash

Midlife can bring financial considerations that, for some, were distant considerations in our earlier decades. Things like: Are we saving enough for retirement? Do we invest in our current home or will we eventually downsize? Do we put money toward a long-term care plan or our kids' schooling? These are big financial decisions and considerations.

Money is also unpredictable. Vacillating stock markets and COVID made that loud and clear in recent decades. The pandemic may have indeed raised the level of concern over finances in this study because so many of us were blindsided and negatively impacted by COVID-related circumstances. Our jobs, and the steady incomes that once felt so secure, were suddenly put into question due to a highly contagious virus. For some, this financial uncertainty propelled further consideration of how long they should continue to work and if their savings are sufficient.

Finances can further complicate the caregiving situation. Being in the sandwich generation means that some of us simultaneously assist our parents and pay college tuition while also trying to maintain enough for our retirement and future medical needs. On their part, aging parents may feel embarrassed or ashamed when they need assistance from their kids. And many midlife women reported feeling resentful (and then feel guilty from this resentment) when their parents' financial needs cut into their own savings.

Here are a few quotes from interviewees that describe their sandwich experience:

* ❋ "There are so many moving parts. Sometimes it's hard to prioritize who to care for."
* ❋ "I'm a single parent mom working a full-time job. I simply don't have enough time in my day for both parents and my daughter. I live with perpetual guilt."
* ❋ "I'm grieving my father, I'm my mom and son's primary support, and my boyfriend wants more attention. My neck literally hurts from carrying it all."
* ❋ "My mom has dementia and I have seven children and seven grandchildren. I deal with the pressure from all sides by volunteering. It nurtures me."
* ❋ "It's a shit storm."

As we have been advised before every airplane flight takes off, you must first put on your own oxygen mask before you can assist others. I would wager that these instructions are repeated every time we fly, not only for everyone's safety, but because it goes against our instincts, and especially women's instincts, to put our needs first. On and off an airplane, we are only able to effectively tend to the numerous competing demands in our lives if we take care of ourselves, if we are literally breathing.

As one wise interviewee shared, "I'm number one on the list. I learned the hard way, and I mean hard way, that if I don't prioritize my needs then no one gets me." Amen, sister!

Lower Ranking Areas of Concern:

This chapter would not be complete without addressing physical appearance and hormonal (i.e., perimenopause and menopause) changes, two areas that ranked unexpectedly low in our relative concerns.

The findings are surprising because they are materially different from the stereotypes and assumptions about midlife women. Menopause is virtually synonymous with midlife. We instinctively associate the two. Furthermore, were one to gauge our concerns by the marketing of products targeted at us, you would think that hot flashes and wrinkles are the bane of our existence. Yes, those can be major issues, but *we* know that is not the entire story, and my research supports this reality.

Physical Appearance Changes

Surprisingly, only eighteen percent of the survey respondents rated appearance as a very concerning area, a number far fewer than those very concerned with the issues discussed above.

This does not imply that we are necessarily happy with our changing appearance nor that we don't desire to look our best. Many women shared their frustration with weight gain and most of us would love to do without our increasing wrinkles, drier everything, those red cherry dots, etc. *Rather, this finding speaks to the more pressing challenges of losses, physical decline, and the sandwich demands.*

The relatively lower ranking of physical appearance, as a challenge, could also be related to some of the midlife gifts I will discuss in Chapter 7, such as increased confidence and comfort in our skin. It is possible that when we are more at ease in our overall being, we are less focused on our external appearance.

So yes, in midlife, like at every point in our lives, we want to look our best. But we are not as vain as we are culturally portrayed, and other challenges weigh more heavily on us.

Hormonal Changes

Hormonal changes during midlife include an erratic decline in estrogen and progesterone production. This hormonal chaos is the source of many of the challenges of perimenopause and menopause (e.g., hot flashes and night sweats, vaginal dryness, uterine bleeding, etc.). The impact of these hormonal shifts can cause anything from minor inconveniences to life-changing disruptions.

Though menopause (i.e., hormonal changes) *is* an indisputable challenge of midlife, for this sample of women, it does not rank in our top five very concerning challenges. Only seventeen percent of the respondents rated hormonal changes as "very concerning," and it was near the bottom of the overall ranking of concerns. Even accounting for age, hormonal changes did not rank as challenging as death and loss, sandwich demands, and other issues on our plates.[15]

Wait, what? Aren't those dreaded hot flashes the defining feature of middle age? It was the only thing I ever heard of in connection to midlife. In fact, I had heard so much about menopause that it became this big "thing" in my head. Would I wake up in the middle of the night dripping sweat? Would I gain ten pounds that would be impossible to shed? Was that one?! Did I just have a hot flash?

There are a few reasons why those dreaded hot flashes and other hormone-related challenges may have ranked lower in our relative concerns. As illustrated earlier in this chapter, some of our menopause-related physical challenges are likely captured under the health/physical decline category, the issue of upmost concern. Even

---

[15]   See Appendix 2

in the shifting climate, women are still not routinely educated that many of their physical ailments may be a result of hormonal fluctuations. Should women have appreciated the connections between some of their physical challenges and menopause, this category could have ranked significantly higher.

Secondly, as discussed below, there is tremendous variability in women's menopausal experiences. For some it is a hiccup and for others, a colossal challenge. This gamut of experiences may have also contributed to its lower relative ranking of concerns, as it is not universally problematic. Furthermore, menopause may be a focal point during a portion of midlife—when the hormonal chaos is most extreme—but less of an issue in the latter part of midlife.

Hot flashes and many other less talked about hormone-related symptoms are absolutely a challenging aspect of midlife, regardless of their ranking. *The bigger takeaway is that perimenopause and menopause are happening within the larger backdrop of our total midlife experience. They are but one of a number of significant challenges.*

The Many Menopausal Experiences

Women's individual experiences of menopause are all over the map. In fact, Tina said that she spent a decade fearing what menopause would be like for her, only to be underwhelmed when she actually went through it. Judy said that she had no clue she was in menopause until her doctor ran labs as part of an annual physical. She was shocked at the news, as she had no discernible symptoms. A few other women I interviewed stated that menopause was "not a big deal."

On the other end of the spectrum were a portion of interviewees who said that menopause was downright brutal; that it literally took over their lives and sometimes even their ability to maintain their jobs. Leah's symptoms were so physically and emotionally debilitating that she had difficulty functioning at work and ended up selling her business.

Regardless of the extent and intensity of one's individual symptoms, there was almost universal frustration over the lack of information about menopause.

Frustration with Lack of Information

What made hormonal challenges worse for many women I interviewed were the entirely unexpected symptoms that they did not know were menopause related, such as difficulties with concentration or memory lapses. Some (including me) worried that these challenges reflected symptoms of early-onset dementia or other neurological problems. Doctors seldom explained that these problems could be a function of lower hormone levels. Frustration regarding confusing, and even contradictory, information about treatment was another common complaint, resulting in women taking the lead in researching treatment options.

Many women I interviewed were forthright about being unprepared for the sexual changes associated with menopause—lower libido, decreased arousal, vaginal dryness, and painful intercourse. These challenges directly impacted the quality and quantity of their sexual activity. Alicia said that she had to redefine intimacy with her husband separate from the physical component. We (and our partners) would have been thrilled if our doctors had not only prepared us for these changes but also offered treatment options, such as vaginal estrogen.

The End of Fertility

Yet another challenging aspect, for some women, was the implication of menopause: the end of our ability to bear children. For those women who could not have children, menopause permanently and heartbreakingly closed a door to their dreams. Orna said she would tear up whenever she saw a pregnant woman because the vision reminded her that she could no longer have children. Cindy said that her body was her "superpower." She felt devoid of her powers when she entered menopause.

In sum, women's despair about the implications of menopause and the many unexpected, worrisome, and painful symptoms was aggravated by the lack of information and medically directed treatment options for these common challenges, a theme addressed more extensively in Chapter 11.

Summary

Taking in all of these conversations, we see a number of overarching points about our collective menopausal experiences:

1. Though not a highest-ranking concern for this sample, menopause is nevertheless a significant component of midlife. Its lower ranking speaks to the significant challenges of the other issues, not the reduced challenge of menopause.

2. Some of the physical challenges of menopause are likely captured under the "health and physical decline" category, which ranked as our foremost concern. As a result, menopause may actually be a higher-ranking concern.

3. Menopausal symptoms are far more extensive than the presence of hot flashes. There are a number of additional physical, cognitive, and emotional ramifications of lower hormone levels that are less known to many women and not addressed by most medical providers.

4. There are tremendous individual variations in terms of our menopausal symptoms and their respective impact on our lives.

5. Common symptoms, such as memory decline, brain fog, and anxiety were unexpected and seldom appreciated as possibly due to menopause. This caused some women to fear they had unique, unrelated medical problems.

6. Many women feel diminished, unheard, and even pathologized by their medical providers (in particular male practitioners) which caused additional emotional pain.

7. Menopause occurs concurrently with other losses, physical changes, caretaking demands, and more. It impacts the totality of our menopausal experience and our capacity to tend to these simultaneous challenges.

8. The treatment options are confusing and even contradictory. The significant advances in the benefits of hormone replacement therapy are not widely circulated or known by the majority of doctors.

The Bottom Line

Midlife is flush with aging-related challenges, several of which are unique to women. Though we knew that many of these changes, like losing loved ones and our physical decline, would eventually happen, when they appeared in midlife, we were still surprised. We expected menopause, but not its extent of symptoms, how doctors may respond, or the lack of treatment guidance. We knew, even if we did not want to accept it, that our parents would pass but we did not expect our friends or siblings to die so young. And few of us considered the toll of caretaking. Death, loss, physical decline, sandwich demands, menopause, appearance changes, and more are *all* aspects of the challenging midlife landscape.

Fortunately, as difficult as these issues are, they are only part of midlife. In Chapter 7, we will dive into the welcoming, exciting, and oft-overlooked gifts that also come with age. But first, let's explore how using SOFTT can help manage and soften the midlife challenges.

CHAPTER 6

APPLYING SOFTT TO THE CHALLENGES

"For fast-acting relief, try slowing down."

—Lily Tomlin

It was less than forty-eight hours after my mom unexpectedly died and I needed a dress for her funeral. (When I got the news that she was being rushed into surgery, I was so distraught that I threw random clothes into a suitcase and booked the first flight to New Orleans.) I drove to one of my mom's favorite stores, the now-shuttered SteinMart, and purchased the first black dress I saw. As I exited the store in a daze, I could not remember where I parked, much less whose car I drove. With tears streaming down my face, I walked up and down the aisles of the parking lot, not even seeing the cars. When I became literally blinded by my tears, I stepped onto the sidewalk, leaned against the wall, put my head in my hands, and sobbed.

A light touch on my arm startled me back to the present. I looked up and saw a kind looking, older woman who said in a New Orleans drawl, "Let's sit down for a second, baby." She helped me sit and waited until I collected myself.

"What's the matter, darlin'?" she gently asked.

"My mom just died and I can't find my car," I replied.

"Oh, I'm so sorry, baby, I lost my mama too. That's a hard one," she said.

"I can't believe it," I said, beginning to come back to my senses. "I didn't even get to say goodbye…my poor dad," I said with tears welling up again. "And I can't find my car." She was listening so intently that I did not realize she had placed her arm around me. I rested my head on her shoulder, comforted by this stranger's gentle embrace, aware now of my deep sadness and fatigue, and the heaviness in my body.

"It's gonna be okay, baby," she said. "It's hard when you lose your mama but it's gonna be okay."

I nodded, feeling a bit relieved by her reassurance. I'm not sure if it was one minute or ten before I lifted my head back up, and again scanned the parking lot.

"Now, are you ready to go find that car?" she asked.

"Yes, thank you," I replied as she gently helped me up and escorted me through the parking lot.

This woman, this angel, who appeared in a moment of profound sorrow, will always hold a special place in my heart. I do not know her name and will never see her again in this lifetime, but I will always remember her generous, compassionate help through that moment of despair.

In retrospect, I realized that what we did together was SOFTT. My angel helped me to slow down, observe my thoughts and emotions, feel into my sorrow, and she offered infinite tenderness. And then, we easily found my car.

Choosing to Respond

Challenges are an inevitable part of midlife, of being human. And though we cannot control their appearance, we do have a say in how we respond to them.

One of the most brilliant and inspiring people to teach about this choice is Viktor Frankl. He was an Austrian-Jewish neurologist, psychologist, professor, and author. He was also a Holocaust survivor. In 1942, at the age of thirty-seven, Frankl and his family were sent to the Theresienstadt concentration camp, his first of four different camps. Over the next three years, his mother, father, and brother were murdered by the Nazis. Frankl knew suffering in its rawest, cruelest form.

Among Frankl's many extraordinary offerings is his book, *Man's Search for Meaning*. One of the core theories it presents is that even when everything it taken from a person, including in circumstances as horrific as the Holocaust, we still retain the ability to choose how to respond. This idea is captured in the famous quote, "Between stimulus and response there is a space. In that space is our power to choose our response. In our response lies our growth and our freedom."[16] Frankl (and Buddhism) maintain that suffering is an unavoidable part of life, and that our freedom is based on how we choose to respond to it.

SOFTT provides the "space" mentioned in the above quote. Beginning with slowing down and culminating with tuning in, SOFTT widens the space between our stimuli (our challenges) and response (how we deal with them). SOFTT does not take away pain. It is not designed for that, though it may soften our experience of pain. What it provides is mental and emotional room for a wider,

---

[16] Though attributed to Frankl, the Victor Frankl Institute notes that the origin of this quote was indirectly attributed to him.

deeper exploration of our challenges and, with that, in Frankl's words, "the power to choose our response."

SOFTT is best applied with an open, curious mind. Any part of the process can engender resistance, as the steps are not natural practices. Most of us have not been trained to slow down, to observe our thoughts and emotions, and to intentionally lean in to the physical experience.

Quite the opposite: we are conditioned to busyness, avoidance, and trying to fix things we do not like. By approaching SOFTT with openness and curiosity, it will offset our habitual, conditioned, insufficient ways of responding.

Examples of Applying SOFTT

I have chosen the top two midlife challenges (loss and physical decline) to illustrate how to apply SOFTT.

As you read the examples, remember that there are countless flavors of ways these and other challenges manifest in our unique lives. If the example does not apply to you, change the scenario to fit your situation. The practices embedded in SOFTT are what I am intending to exemplify. And, they can be applied to any circumstance, including those that are less extreme.

Scenario 1: Loss

Grief is a natural outcome of loss. It is an intense, powerful, and sometimes beautiful experience. I would like to believe that the depth of grief we experience is commensurate with the depth of love we have for whomever or whatever it is we lost. Queen Elizabeth once said,

"Grief is the price we pay for love." And sometimes, in the course of being present to our grief, we can taste that love in a palpable way.

If you have experienced grief, you know firsthand that it is not linear. It can appear expectedly, such as on birthdays and anniversaries, and also pop up quite unexpectedly, such as when we hear a song or are struck with a memory that reminds us of this person. Elisabeth Kubler-Ross, who wrote extensively on the stages of grief, said the following: "The reality is that you will grieve forever. You will not 'get over' the loss of a loved one; you will learn to live with it. You will heal, and you will rebuild yourself around the loss you have suffered. You will be whole again, but you will never be the same. Nor should you be the same, nor would you want to."[17]

SOFTT can be applied to grief, regardless of where you are in the grief journey. It can help when you are in the midst of intense sorrow and confusion, as I was when I could not find my car, or in less-extreme moments of sadness or anger. This process can be done repeatedly throughout an hour, day, months, or years.

> **The SOFTT process can also help** to process grief in the following areas beyond deaths of loved ones: empty nest, divorce, job loss/retirement, changes/ends of relationships, loss in parent or elders' functioning, invisibility, pet deaths, and any other experience of loss.

For this example, I will apply SOFTT to the death of a loved one. However, you can practice with any loss that has brought you

---

[17] Kubler-Ross, E and Kessler, D. *On Grief and Grieving: Finding the Meaning of Grief Through the Five Stages of Loss.* Scribner, 2005.

despair. Refer to the shaded box for a list of some common midlife scenarios around loss.

SET-UP. Find a quiet place to sit, where you will not be interrupted for at least ten minutes. Turn off (and over) your phone if it is nearby. Think of a person you have lost. They may be passed or alive. Bring an image of this person to both mind and heart. If it proves too difficult to imagine this person, find a picture of him or her and look at it for at least a minute. You may even want to have a picture nearby for reference. Drink in this image. Allow your loved one's essence to come into your heart, regardless of what emotions it evokes. If tears surface, allow them to flow. There is no rush or pressure. SOFTT is a gentle process by design. When you are ready, turn to Step 1.

Step 1 – Slow Down and Breathe. Close your eyes and take at least three deep, cleansing breaths. If you can, breathe from your diaphragm for three to six seconds on the inhalation. Notice how your chest and belly rise as they fill with air. Then exhale for six to eight seconds, noticing how your chest and belly relax as the air leaves your body. Be sure to fully exhale. Many of us shorten our exhalations in our eagerness to begin the next inhalation.

Next, allow your breath to settle into a natural, unforced rate and rhythm. Focus on the rising and falling of your chest with your breath, instead of any thoughts.

As you simply sit and breathe, notice whether your body is settling as you create some space from your grief. This could take seconds or minutes. It depends entirely on you and the situation. Commonly, the more intense your emotions, the more time it takes for the body to slow down. Take as many breath cycles as you want and need. When you feel some measure of settling, turn to Step 2.

Step 2 – Observe and Release Your Thoughts and Emotions. From this safe distance, notice and release any thoughts and emotions coming up for you. If it helps, you can imagine you are watching yourself on a movie screen. Some of your thoughts and emotions may be expected and familiar, and others quite unexpected and unfamiliar. You may observe several conflicting thoughts and emotions arise at the same time—confusion and relief, for example. That's okay.

Do your best not to deny, judge, or engage with any beliefs or emotions that arise. Allow yourself the precious space to just take stock, and not get caught up in the temptation to answer any questions that may surface.

As you observe these thoughts and emotions, release them into air and see them fading like a cloud in the sky. Alternatively, you can imagine putting these thoughts and feelings in a box, and gently closing the lid, with the knowledge that you can choose to revisit them later.

Allow them all to flow and release without restraint. Take your time.

Here are some thoughts that can surface in the face of grief:

* This cannot be real.
* How can he or she be gone?
* I cannot believe I will never see him or her again.
* It is too painful.
* Who will I turn to for ____?
* Why him? Her?
* I wish I had said or done _____.
* Why didn't he or she take better care of herself?
* I'm an orphan now.
* This isn't fair.

The range of emotions that may arise surrounding loss can include:

* Sorrow
* Overwhelm
* Anger
* Numbness
* Relief
* Loneliness
* Confusion

When you have observed as many of the thoughts and emotions present in the moment as you can, move to Step 3.

Step 3 – Feel into Your Physical Sensations. In this step, you transition from being a distant observer of your experience to bringing your full attention to your physical experience. You already know how to notice body sensations, such as twinges of hunger, low back pain, or your heart racing in excitement. So, for now, gently attune to your physical experience, to your muscles and organs and skin, and feel the various sensations.

Is there tension in your eyes, neck, or shoulders?

Are your jaws tight or achy?

Do your legs feel heavy?

Is your belly jangled or nauseous?

If it is difficult for you to identify distinct sensations, try a scan of your body.

To scan your body, start at your head and zero in on your scalp. Then glide your attention down to your eyes, jaws, neck, shoulders, belly, back, legs, and feet. Simply be present to any physical sensations you notice, without judgment.

If you cannot discern individual bodily sensations, bring your attention to your body as a whole and feel into it. Even numbness has a sensation.

If and when thoughts and emotions re-enter the mix and dominate your attention, imagine gently putting them back in a box and then return to notice your body. The purpose is to be present to your physical, embodied sensations, while keeping the mental chatter and emotions at bay. Continue to scan your bodily sensations for as long as you like or are able. When you are ready, move to Step 4.

Step 4 – Apply Tenderness. Give yourself the same verbal and/ or physical tenderness you would offer others in grief, just as that angel-of-a-woman gave me in the parking lot in New Orleans.

Place your hand on your heart, or wrap your arms around your chest in a self-embrace, and feel into the physically nurturing gesture. Try it for a second, even if it feels awkward. If it is helpful, continue with this comforting physical touch. Next, say gentle words to yourself that capture your real-time experience. "This is really hard," "This hurts," or (one of my teacher's favorites) "There, there," are examples of tender words. Choose words that feel right for you at this moment. Allow the comfort to wash over you. Stay here as long as you like. When you are ready, turn to Step 5.

Step 5 – Tune In to Your Inner Wisdom. This final step is when we tune in to our inner wisdom in order to identify what it is we need, or how we are choosing to respond, in the moment. Avoid "thinking" about the answers. Instead, "listen" with openness and curiosity. What may appear could be very different from what you expected.

Here are a handful of examples of grief-related wisdom that women reported:

* The need for reassurance, support, or guidance; perhaps the urge to reach out to friends who have lost loved ones, or even a therapist

* The necessity to temporarily delegate some responsibilities or take time off of work

* The need to ask for (or be open to receive) help with meals, childcare, errands

* Time for self-care, in the form of more sleep, walks outside, or alone time to process

* The recollection that time with friends, in nature, at church, etc., helped previously

* The memory that you have gone through difficult times in the past and made it through

Now is also the time to revisit any thoughts that need exploration. Some of our thoughts and questions do not have any answers, or at least none that are satisfying. "Why him?" is an example of an unanswerable inquiry, especially when you are in the midst of intense grief. Often, focusing on "why" leads to more distress.

But some inner inquiries do have answers, such as who you will call if you need advice or support. This is when you may bring to mind your close friends and relatives who would be honored to support you. No, they are not and will never replace your loved one(s), but they still love you and can provide a degree of comfort.

If you cannot remember any thoughts, that is fine too. It means that they are not important in the moment.

Wrap-Up. Before you leave this process, take stock of how you feel now compared to how you felt before you began the SOFTT process. Do you feel any shift, even a subtle one? If so, what has shifted? Was there any aspect of this process that was particularly helpful? Maybe it was when you allowed the jumbled thoughts to release or perhaps it was when you placed your hand on your heart. Remember that and use it as a go-to tool.

And if you feel the same as before you started, that too is okay. Congratulate yourself for your effort. Please do not put any pressure or expectation on yourself to feel differently. The goal is not to change your thoughts or feelings. It is to be tenderly present to your "right now" experience, and, in this softer space, to increase your likelihood to respond, rather than react, to your loss.

> As you traverse your grief journey, carry SOFTT in your back pocket, along with a memory of a loved one that makes you smile.

Scenario 2: Physical Decline and Changes

Physical decline and changes are often the most irrefutable signs that we are aging, that our bodies have begun to bear the marks of time. All physical decline is hard. Whether it is our waning hearing or vision, acute or chronic pain, or feeling as if we are the Tin Man in *The Wizard of Oz* who needs to be oiled every morning, bodily decline is an undeniable challenge.

Here's an example of applying SOFTT to physical decline:

SET-UP. Bring to mind an aspect of your physicality that is a challenge. Perhaps it is a body part, such as your eyes or knees. Or maybe it is a challenge with a feature of your physical appearance, such as thinning skin, drooping eyelids, or a softer belly. Reflect for a moment on how this challenge impacts your life. Does it affect your self-esteem, what clothes you wear, or which activities you choose to take part in or avoid? Once you have clearly delineated the physical challenge, move to Step 1.

Step 1 – Slow Down and Breathe. Slow down and take at least three deep breaths. Aim to inhale for three to six seconds, and exhale for five to seven seconds. Take as much time as you need to slow and regulate your breath. When you are ready, move to Step 2.

Step 2 – Observe Your Thoughts and Emotions. Nonjudgmentally (this part is essential) and objectively observe the array of thoughts and emotions surrounding your body part or physical decline. Allow all of them to flow and release freely, without denying or engaging with them. When we engage with our thoughts, we are no longer an observer; we are in a direct inner conversation. If this happens, simply step back and return to an observer mode, as if you are watching yourself on a movie screen. Take as much time as needed to observe any thoughts and emotions that are present and then release them into the air, behind an imaginary door, or in a box.

Here are some thoughts women shared related to their physical challenges:

* Aging sucks.
* I hate that I can no longer jog, ski, play pickleball, etc.

* I look like an old lady.
* What if I'll never be able to _____ again?
* I'm going to gain weight without being able to _____.
* I'm too young to feel this fragile.
* I never thought this would happen so soon.

Some feelings associated with physical decline include:

* Sadness
* Fear
* Worry
* Vulnerability
* Anger
* Frustration
* Anxiety

When you feel like you have a handle on your mental content and emotions, move to Step 3.

Step 3 – Feel into Your Physical Sensations. If you have physical pain secondary to a body part, cautiously and curiously explore how the pain feels in your body. Is it sharp with edges or is it diffuse? Is it chronic or intermittent? Does it change in seconds, minutes? If your shoulders, neck, or low back hurt, linger on these sensations (nothing bad will happen) and notice the nuances of discomfort. All the while, stay clear of internally shouting, "Ouch!" or "This sucks." Should those thoughts resurface, and they likely will, intentionally and gently put them in the box for the time being.

If you are not currently in pain, drop into whatever sensations are present. If there is an aspect of your physical appearance that upsets you, feel into any sensations around that part of your body. Do you feel heavy from sorrow, or tense from anger? Simply feel whatever is going on in your body in this very moment. When you are ready, move to Step 4.

Step 4 – Tenderness. Give your body and heart the tenderness it needs, via physical touch and words. In this scenario, you can either place your hand on your heart or on the area that hurts, is deteriorating, or that you dislike, and comfort that place with your touch. Then add specific words of self-compassion, such as "It's a bummer that I cannot dance or run or lift weights anymore," "It's rough to always be in pain," or "It is hard for me to look older."

Stay here until you experience the essence of this step. Many of us try to manage the physical sensations of pain with medications, treatment, or rehabilitation but are less likely to address the emotional pain associated with physical decline or appearance changes. Our bodies and hearts are intertwined. When we tend to the heart, we also help our bodies.

When you are ready, proceed to the last step.

Step 5 – Tune In to Your Inner Wisdom. Invite your inner wisdom to surface and listen to what it reveals pertaining to this challenge. What do you hear? Examples of inner wisdom in this realm could be:

* ❋ I need to be kinder to my body.
* ❋ I am too judgmental of myself.
* ❋ I have made it through other physically challenging times.
* ❋ I know I can and will adapt.

Your wisdom may also reveal:

* An awareness of what I *can* physically do
* An appreciation of the parts of my appearance I still like
* An awareness of how I "see" and treat others with physical challenges and aging appearances

Wrap-Up. Having moved through these five steps, pause to explore if you think or feel differently with regard to this challenge. Was any aspect helpful? Has anything shifted in your relationship to this challenge? Add any answers to these inquiries to your bank of inner wisdom and remember to turn to it again and again. And if nothing has changed, do not worry. It is a process, not a destination.

Where else to use SOFTT

SOFTT can be applied to many other challenges. The circumstances need not be as extreme as the examples above. SOFTT can help when we fumble during a presentation, when we cannot button up our favorite jeans, and when we grapple with existential questions such as "What's next?" or "Is this all there is?"

I use SOFTT when I am agitated for no discernable reason. I had one of those moments, not too long ago, while driving to the gym. So, I pulled my car over to the side of the road to practice SOFTT. Within minutes, I discovered some latent thoughts that contributed to my mood. When I observed them, leaned into the sensation in my body, and gave myself a dose of self-compassion, my mood shifted. My workout was enjoyable and I was definitely more pleasant to be around than in my prior state. Softness is that subtle, gentle shift in the face of any confusing or difficult moment or passage.

Bottom Line

When we were younger, most of us thought little of the midlife challenges we now face. Even when we knew irrefutably that loved ones would pass and our bodies would inevitably decline, many of us did not appreciate how these challenges would impact us, until they were at our gates.

To embrace midlife challenges with SOFTT is courageous. It is choosing to ride the waves of the storm rather than to swim against them. SOFTT does not mean we like their existence. Nor does it imply we should not seek help for our challenges or strive to be our best selves. In contrast, it is opting to appreciate the fullness of our challenges, and to go through them in a safe, gentle manner. A friend recently said, "I'm facing midlife like I did labor pains. I am riding them out rather than fighting them." Though SOFTT does not end with the birth of a child, the intensity of our pain lessens. And our labor, our journey through it, can be more gracious and spacious than we ever imagined.

Fortunately, challenges are only part of this season. Midlife is also awash in gifts. Yet, we sometimes lose sight of the wonderful aspects of these decades because the difficulties can consume our focus. When we do this, we miss out on so many of the "goodies" of midlife, many of which can only come with age.

The next chapter explores in more detail these wonderful, often-overlooked gifts of the middle. Read and enjoy. I am certain you will see yourself, and your growth, in many of them.

Chapter 7

MIDLIFE GIFTS

"I've gathered strength behind my years, I owned them, I've earned them, I've deserved them, I have a right to have them."

—Sally Field

It was a chilly December afternoon in 2020. Jackie and I were winding down the portion of the interview discussing her midlife challenges. We had talked about everything from her mom's dementia to her concern (and secret intrigue) with her son's increasing "spiritual journeys" with psychedelic mushrooms.

"So, Jackie, let's shift gears from the challenges. Have you experienced any positive aspects of midlife? Do you feel that midlife has any gifts or benefits?"

"Ahh, yes, so many," Jackie replied with a long exhale and a grin forming. Even through Zoom, I noticed the muscles in her face and shoulders relax. "Despite all the shit I described, life is so much better. I don't waste my time worrying about stupid stuff anymore, like if my house is nice enough for company or what this person thinks of me. I'm me and if you don't like me, or my house, f*ck it! I save my energy for things that really matters. And even though I have concerns related to my mom and son, I'm still so much less anxious than I used to be."

"How are you both concerned and less anxious?" I asked.

"I worry about the things that deserve worrying, like my mom's health, rather than worry about everything. I used to stress out to the point of insomnia every time I had to try a case. (Jackie is a federal prosecutor.) I would lie in bed at night, trying to pick out the perfect suit to wear and rehearse my opening statement over and over again—even in my dreams. Now, I prepare the best I can and go to sleep. It's okay if it's not perfect and if I don't look perfect. I don't beat myself up like I used to. I don't know if it's because I am surer of myself or if bigger issues have given me perspective."

"That's great," I said with a smile. "Shall we move on to the next question?"

"Wait—I got a tattoo last year for my forty-fifth birthday!" Jackie excitedly said as she moved her wrist up to the camera to display the detailed, colorful image of a sea turtle.

"Beautiful. Why a sea turtle?" I asked.

"I love snorkeling in Hawaii. It's my happy place," she explained. "The turtle reminds me of that when I get stressed. I had wanted one for a long time," Jackie continued, "but was worried it would tarnish my lawyer image and credibility, not to mention what the other moms on the PTA would think." We both laughed. (I, a former PTA president, know that world intimately.) "But now? Who cares! Seriously."

"I get it!" I excitedly replied as I awkwardly lifted my leg toward the camera to show Jackie the purple lotus tattoo on my ankle. "I got this one when I was fifty-five. The color purple has special meaning for me and the lotus reminds me of my spiritual path. It took me a while to get the courage to do something so permanent. I also heard echoes in my head of my father's disdain of tattoos.

I told Jackie my vivid memory of driving to the tattoo parlor. I was excited and nervous and had the thought that my tattoo would represent another adulting step away from my parents' influence on my decisions (despite the fact that both had been deceased for years). It was liberating.

Jackie understood. Our tattoos represented much more than body art; their presence captures our individuality, our courage, our certainty, and our decreased concern with how others would react to our choices.

Jackie's narrative regarding her midlife gifts conveyed a number of common themes. Many of us notice a gradual decrease of our interior battles with anxiety, questioning of our competencies, and preoccupation with others' opinions—these are replaced with more ease, confidence, and comfort in our skin. We don't feel as much need to prove ourselves or to get permission from others for our choices. We know with greater certainty what is and what *is not* important, and have a deeper sense of self-awareness. We have more freedom, literally and figuratively, and unequivocally more wisdom.

I was amazed at how often women were surprised, and then affirmed, when they considered the extent of their midlife gifts. "My shifts happened so subtly and over time that I hadn't really noticed them. But things are different...in a good way," Martha said. Belia shared a similar realization. Until our interview, Belia was unaware of how much less she struggles with what she considered to be lifelong issues around pleasing people and making decisions. She had been too busy taking care of her father to notice her own growth. "They actually *aren't* lifelong issues. I didn't consciously try to change these things in therapy or anything, they just happened over time. That's really cool." "I agree," I replied, "It is cool."

The paragraph below is the exact wording in the survey question on midlife gifts. Before you read the results, I invite you to pause and answer the questions yourself, using the instructions below.

Question 4. Thinking about the past few years (i.e., pre-COVID), how much do these potential midlife benefits ring true for you as compared with your twenties and thirties?

Directions: Rate each of the following categories according to the following scale: Not There (0), Slightly Resonates (1), Moderately Resonates (2), Very Much Resonates (3), or Extremely Resonates (4).

	Category	Your Ranking
1	I'm more comfortable in my skin (i.e., I am generally at ease with myself and when I'm around others)	
2	I know myself better (i.e., likes, dislikes, triggers, behaviors, etc.)	
3	I have more me time (i.e., time for myself)	
4	I don't "sweat the small stuff," (i.e., worry about little things)	
5	My friendships are more fulfilling	
6	I do less "people pleasing"	
7	I have more wisdom, life lessons	
8	I am more emotionally resilient (i.e., recover more quickly from difficult conditions)	
9	It's an opportunity to re-evaluate my life and make changes	
10	Other:	

List your highest-scoring gifts here:

1. _____
2. _____
3. _____

Per the survey respondents, our collective, highest-ranking gifts among the designated categories are:

1. More Wisdom
2. More Self-Awareness
3. More Fulfilling Friendships

Within these three categories, wisdom and self-awareness prevailed as the top two gifts.

Wisdom

Wisdom appears to be a gift that gives generously with age. With every turn around the sun, we encounter new experiences that, in turn, can breed life lessons. And by midlife, we have accumulated decades of experiences and ample opportunities to learn and grow. We have had our share of joys and sorrows, ups and down, trials and tribulations. We have had our hearts broken and we have broken hearts. We have loved and hurt, won and lost, behaved skillfully and unskillfully. We have made good decisions and bad ones. And our wisdom grew through each experience, especially the difficult ones. They are collectively our unique life's teachings.

The survey data supports a direct relationship between wisdom and age, with the experience of greater wisdom steadily increasing over time. There was a statistically significant increase in perceived wisdom from our forties to our fifties and from our fifties to our sixties. This is consistent with Dr. Christian Northrup's assertion that we are most able to access our wisdom after menopause, in part due to hormonal changes.

Embodied Wisdom

I believe that our wisdom not only increases with age but, for many, how we understand it changes over time as well. Our wisdom gradually shifts from our heads to our body; from being thoughts to embodied "knowing." That is, with repeated experience, our accumulated wisdom increasingly takes hold on a visceral level; it becomes part of who we are. We do not have to think as much about certain decisions because we know the answer in our bodies. If we listen to it, or tune in to it during the last step of SOFTT, our inner wisdom can become our inner guide and compass.

Instinctual Wisdom

When I taught risk assessment of criminal offenders to graduate students, I always implored aspiring forensic psychologists to listen to their instincts when talking with their clients—to be aware if the hairs on their arms stands up, if something feels "off," or if there is a disconnect between what they hear and how they feel. Relying on my instincts was not something I learned in graduate school (nor would it fly as data during my courtroom testimony) but it was an invaluable source of information professionally, and continues to be personally.

I believe that our instincts are an aspect of our embodied wisdom. As with all other wisdom, it grows and becomes fine-tuned with age. It is that automatic reaction we feel in our "gut," or other parts of our bodies, that relays information. Whether we choose to heed our instinctual wisdom is another story.

I learned some very hard-earned lessons with regard to *not* honoring my instinctual wisdom. I had served on the board of an organization during a few extremely tumultuous years. The demands on the board members were akin to a part-time job. It was physically, mentally, and emotionally exhausting. When my commitment was over, I told the CEO that I would not be available for another term. This was a difficult conversation because she was a friend and mentor who I knew wanted me to stay on the board. I was shocked by her reaction. She became visibly upset, raised her voice, and implored me to remain for another year. She insisted that the challenges of the preceding year were an anomaly. Though she apologized via email almost immediately, the interaction stayed with me. She was so distressed during our conversation that I backed down and agreed to stay on another term, mostly as a service to her. It was a terrible decision. The organizational situation spiraled even further out of control, as did its demands on my time, my life, and emotional well-being.

There were many lessons I learned from that very dark, long chapter. But perhaps my biggest one was the cost of overriding my instincts. My gut "knew" the better choice was to leave after my term. I heard it, I announced it, but then backed down. I ignored my instinctive wisdom, was swayed by people-pleasing, and used mental rationalizations to convince myself it would be okay. It was not. Since that chapter of my life, I listen to my instincts with much more frequency.

I do not know if instinct increases with age. After all, some kids and animals have amazing instincts. But I do think that we listen to our instincts more closely (except, um, me in the above situation) and are less likely to allow cognitive logic to replace them. And I believe that most of us have learned by now that our instincts are, more often than not, spot-on.

Wisdom of Hardships

Similar to my example above, many interviewees shared that their richest, most impactful life lessons came from enduring difficult situations. Though we do not wish for challenging times, our wisdom grows by going through them and coming out the other side.

Olga said, "My hard knocks became learning opportunities. I appreciate that they built fortitude in me and empathy for others. I judge less, assume less, and question more." An anonymous survey respondent wrote the following: "Life experiences teach you that you will get through hard times. I fall back on the wisdom gained by what I've gotten through."

Consider a past challenging situation, such as a health issue, stressful work situation, or relationship conflict. How did you get through it? What internal and external resources helped you? What did *not* help? And, as you consider your challenging experiences in retrospect, what did you learn? If you pause and ponder these questions, my hunch is that you will uncover many conscious and unconscious lessons you learned along the way, which are now indelible parts of your inner wisdom.

Wisdom grows when we are able to distance ourselves from our experiences, extract their lessons, and see how they fit into our bigger understanding of life. Wisdom grows from living life. Period.

Zen Wisdom

In the Zen community where I practice meditation, we regularly chant this verse during retreats:

Life's teachings are ever-present. May we hear them, receive them, absorb and retain them. May we realize their true meaning.

I love this verse. And, in my latter fifties, I understand the words much more deeply than I did twenty years ago when I first recited them. In my opinion, this profound teaching speaks exactly to the maturation and integration of life's lessons that I propose happens for many in middle age. That is, in midlife, our life experiences (our teachings) become increasingly "heard," "received," "absorbed," and "retained." They are our inner wisdom.

Self-Awareness

Neck-and-neck with wisdom as a top midlife benefit, and closely related, is our sense of increased self-awareness. I see self-awareness as an aspect of wisdom; the part of wisdom that pertains to a clearer understanding of ourselves—our thoughts, feelings, behavior, values and how they impact our choices.

Seeing ourselves clearly and honestly is a tremendous attribute. It enables us to make choices aligned with our authentic self and, hopefully, take ownership of our errors. Self-awareness is also the starting point of healing.

In this sample, interviewees described their self-awareness as knowing with more certainty what makes them happy and what gives them grief, what battles are worth fighting and those that are easier laid to rest, and why certain people press their buttons while they may have no reaction to someone else who may say or do the same thing.

Self-awareness also extends to our greater clarity of our values and priorities. Here's what a few interviewees had to say about theirs:

❋ "I have a much greater certainty in my beliefs, convictions, and opinions than I did in my twenties and thirties and use those as my life compass."

❋ "I am clear about my priorities. I no longer hold back saying what needs to be said or wait for others to call. I pick up the phone and connect. I communicate my feelings with the ones I love and I listen."

❋ "I no longer play the automatic blame game. I reflect more widely and own up to my mistakes."

We also have the awareness, as one interviewee said, "that we have many selves." We can be our patient self and our very impatient self. We can be our compassionate self and just as easily our judgmental self. We can be our kind self and our not-so-kind self. We have a better understanding of why we behave a certain way in one situation and differently in another. This does not mean we are inauthentic or unstable. It means we are human beings composed of "many me's," a term I learned from Elizabeth Hamilton, one of my first Zen teachers.

Greater self-awareness can also open the gates to sudden insights or discoveries—aha moments.

"Aha" Moments

I vividly remember a big "aha" I had at a meditation retreat nineteen years ago. It was perhaps the third or fourth retreat I had ever attended. It began at 5:45 a.m. and ended at nine p.m., so I was barely home. Because my kids were one and three at the time, the teachers granted leniency from the strict schedule in order to visit or call them. That meant I occasionally missed or arrived late to meditation blocks.

I was convinced, by nothing but my sheer imagination, that a woman sitting across from me, whom I did not know but was clearly a seasoned meditator, had negative judgments about my sporadic attendance. As someone who really likes to be liked, this did not sit well with me. So rather than feel the discomfort of her (imagined) negative opinions of me, I decided I did not like her.

Why? Here was the "aha" moment. Because, I eventually understood, if I beat her to the punch and rejected her, it seemed like it would matter less what she thought of me. (Not that we had uttered one word or even made eye contact!) In the stillness of the retreat, I realized that I was pre-emptively rejecting her to offset the potential pain of not being liked. Furthermore, I realized I had used this strategy throughout my life.

I was a bit stunned by this epiphany. Not only with how much I valued being liked but also the mental games I would automatically play to avoid the sting of rejection. It was an important and helpful revelation. It allowed me to refrain from using this strategy and pushed me to explore why being liked is so important to me. That awareness was the starting point of my growth in this area. I grew as I challenged my efforts to always be liked or to proactively reject those whom I imagined dislike me (both of which are impossible, anyway). Those strategies were Band-Aids to cover up a deeper pain of feeling "not enough." This personal insight lives within me.

As a postscript, my fear-based imagining of what the woman was actually thinking was completely off. When the retreat was over, she told me she overheard me mentioning my young daughters and the modified retreat schedule. Whenever I was absent, she imagined this beautiful reunion between me and my children. I, with embarrassment, shared my version of what I imagined was going on in her mind. She laughed. She is lovely. We still practice together at retreats and sometimes reminisce about this first interaction.

Examples of Self-Awareness in Midlife

By her forties, Stella had manifested society's prescription for "arrival": marriage, kids, a house, successful career, "stuff," etc. Yet Stella was unhappy. She had the insight that those very "arrival" indicators were contributing to her unhappiness. Although she had a successful career as an attorney, it was not her heart's desire. She also realized that her large home and material possessions were paradoxically "suffocating" her, as was her husband. As soon as she began to pare down her possessions, she felt wildly liberated. When Stella listened to her heart, rather than society's prescription, happiness began to unfold. She is now single and works as a diversity and inclusion expert.

Deanna said it took two decades and three divorces for her to finally realize that she is happiest when alone. Even after her third divorce, she honed in on her choice of partners, and her capacity to be a partner, as the source of her failed marriages. Until, after some honest soul searching, she had the epiphany, the "aha," that she is most happy when unattached.

Carla realized that her "imposter syndrome" relative to her self-confidence was an identity she carried with her since her twenties when she was less sure of herself. She became aware, at age forty-one, that this story is no longer true. She realized that she is indeed the confident, competent, independent woman she thought she was pretending to be—and that she could drop the imposter storyline.

Gayle, an interviewee from Colorado, provided a great way for us to end the discussion of this topic when she said, "With wisdom and self-awareness, I'm now the best version of myself." That's definitely a gift to be savored.

More Fulfilling Friendships

Friendships in midlife are wonderful. Though we may not have as many as we want, the ones we do have tend to be treasures. And these precious relationships are more than a source of joy; our girlfriends are our primary resource during challenging times. According to the survey data, we turn to our friends more than therapists, self-help books, mentors, and spiritual practices to help us through rough patches.

To have close girlfriends at any point in our lives is a gift, but there is a quality to these more mature relationships that either did not or could not exist in our adolescence, and even young adulthood.

Quality of Midlife Friendships

In our younger decades, our friendships had a different function. They helped us find ourselves and provided a sense of belonging. We needed them to separate from (and complain about) our parents, to sit next to at lunch, and to share our secrets. They helped steady us in the turbulent adolescent waters.

Though these youthful friendships were extremely important, they were not without their challenges. There were fights, hurt feelings, "stolen" boyfriends and girlfriends, betrayed secrets, and exclusive cliques, any of which could make these friendships painful. I don't think most of this was intentional. To me, these dynamics reflected the tumult, insecurity, and uncertainty of our younger years. For some, these patterns continued, though more subtly, into our young adulthood.

But as we aged and matured, the nature of these relationships matured as well. They became more steady, solid, and intimate. The depth of many of these friendships mirrors the depth of our significant life experiences. By this time in our lives, we have all known

121

great joy and deep pain. When we share the rawness and vulnerability of these experiences, it can breed a depth of intimacy previously unimaginable. Just look at two women in a room who discover that they have both had a mastectomy, have a parent with dementia, or lost a child. They do not need to utter a word to feel the unspoken bond. An understanding nod speaks volumes.

I have a group of girlfriends I met two decades ago, when our children were kindergarteners. We adore each other. We have shared many emotions and many milestones, both of ourselves and our kids. We had collective angst over which teacher our child would get, if they would make friends, and how they would fare academically. We commiserated when our kids had their feelings hurt, lost a school election, or contracted lice (ugh, I'm itching just thinking about it!). And, we celebrated their birthdays, accolades, and more recently, college graduations.

During the entire time, we supported one another through our own joys and sorrows. In addition to our annual, highly anticipated "Moms and Mimosas Hike" on the first day of school, we have been there for each other through surgeries, milestone birthday celebrations, and divorces. We have customized "team" T-shirts in honor of one friend's repeat fight with breast cancer and in memory of one we lost. The depth of these relationships reflects the depth of these shared experiences.

Fulfilling midlife friendships are not necessarily based on a long history. A few years ago, I was invited by a friend to join a group she was forming comprised of women she believed to be her wisest friends. I had tried a few women's groups over the years, and even attempted to start my own, but for various reasons, none of them lasted. I accepted this invitation because I liked my friend, I did not know most of the women, and because the majority of us were meeting for the first time.

Though it took a little time to find our groove, we all stayed and love our group. Because of where we are in life, our conversations primarily pertain to us and our midlife evolution, as opposed to our kids and our sharing quickly became deep, vulnerable, and supportive. I attribute the depth of our conversations not only to the specific women in the group but also to our maturity. I love this group in a different way than those that have a long history, and our closeness is a testament to how quickly intimacy can form at this stage of our lives.

So, if you are feeling isolated in midlife, consider joining or starting a group. Having a space where you can share, listen, or "just be" is like penicillin for loneliness, overwhelm, and disconnection. Invite one or two of your friends over for wine (or tea) and ask them to bring along a few of theirs. You never know where it may lead.

Friendships and Mortality

Awareness of our mortality also impacts how we spend our precious time. That is, we increasingly appreciate that our time on Earth is finite and become more selective about with whom we choose to spend it. Many of us phase out draining or one-way friendships and save our coveted free time for more satisfying ones. Unlike some of the obligatory or convenient friendships of our younger years, midlife relationships are (mostly) by choice.

Shelly shared that she did "a friendship sweep" after her mother passed. "Something changed after she died. I had no tolerance for certain friends. One was so moody that I never knew who I was going to see. When my mom died, I realized that I didn't want those kinds of people in my life anymore." Brooke had the same realization when her mom passed. "I cleaned my house of some friends."

Katie said, "I can see death at fifty so I'm not f*cking around. I want to leave interactions feeling inspired and turned on, and that includes with my family. I've got no room or interest for relationships of convenience."

Here are some ways the interviewees described their present friendships:

- ❋ "They lift me up and bring me joy."
- ❋ "There is a mutual give and take. We both initiate, make plans, and call each other."
- ❋ "I can be myself and know I won't be judged."
- ❋ "They are honest and reliable."
- ❋ "They accept me exactly as I am."
- ❋ "One hundred percent of me wants to be with them. There's no ambivalence."

No wonder midlife women view our friendships as a top gift. They are real, supportive, and deeply fulfilling.

Other Gifts

I cannot conclude this chapter without mention of some of the many other gifts highlighted throughout my research. Within the survey categories, "less people pleasing," "more comfort in our skin," and "more resilience" ranked very closely to "more fulfilling friendships."

Each of these shifts reflects not only our maturation, but also our overall ease of being, our increased tendency to please ourselves over others, and our ability to more easily bounce back from challenges. Collectively, they also contribute to a greater sense of self and authenticity.

The interviewees also mentioned gifts that were not listed as categories in the survey. Related to "comfort in our skin," several women discussed feeling more at peace and grounded. Many feel less driven by guilt, put less pressure on themselves, and accept more of their imperfections. Our greater self-acceptance also tends to spill into our perception of others. That is, many women talked about being less judgmental, more forgiving, and simultaneously more compassionate and patient toward others.

Take a moment to savor some inspirational interviewee quotes about aging:

* ❋ "I have a greater sense of peace."
* ❋ "I am more detached from my chaotic thoughts so I have more inner spaciousness."
* ❋ "I don't feel like I'm winging it anymore."
* ❋ "I roll with life more easily."
* ❋ "I can say no without feeling anxious."
* ❋ "I feel more of a relaxed presence, a loosening of the vigilance."
* ❋ "I look at everything through a softer lens. I see more shades of gray, as opposed to only black and white."
* ❋ "This stage of life is like a homecoming, after a long journey, of finally feeling, without a doubt, that I am beautiful, loveable, and worthy."

Ann Landers, the twentieth-century advice columnist, accurately captured most of us when she said, "At age twenty, we worry about what others think of us. At age forty, we don't care what they think of us. At age sixty, we discover they haven't been thinking of us at all."

Confidence

Confidence was another trait several women discussed as related to age. I am not certain whether increased confidence is a contributor or a byproduct of the gifts we've been discussing. Perhaps we are more confident because we are more comfortable in our skin and resilient—or perhaps our greater comfort in our skin helps us feel more confident.

For several women I interviewed, their increased confidence is most evident in the workplace. They, and I would presume many of us, have achieved expertise in their chosen field of work, especially those who have worked in the same vocation for decades. We can speak of our industry as experts because we are. We know our worth, professionally and personally, which relieves us of the need to demonstrate our value to others. It is intrinsic. As one interviewee remarked, "There's value in me. I don't have to try so hard."

Less Fear

Less fear was another theme that came up in the interviews. "I'm not in fight or flight anymore," said one, and "I'm not so scared of life and what's to come," shared another. A different woman captured this sentiment when she said, "I could finally stop running."

To expand on that thread, several women mentioned being less fearful of God, of religious tenets, and even of death. This topic came up while I interviewed my dear friend Ginger in person. "I'm not afraid of death," she said. "When it's my time to go, it's my time to go. What kind of life is it if you're always afraid of death?" Ginger passed away a year after our interview, at the age of sixty-four, from an unexpected and very brief battle with cancer. I miss her and am happy that the end of her too-short life was not plagued with fears of death.

Fear consumes a lot of physical and emotional energy, energy that is then not available elsewhere. I believe that with less fear, there is more room to live. I will close with a quote shared by one of our interviewees, which visually speaks to the expansiveness available with less fear: "I'm doing a swan dive with my eyes open instead of cannonball with my eyes closed." Ah…

The Bottom Line

There are so many overt and subtle gifts of midlife: wisdom, self-awareness, fulfilling friendships, resilience, confidence, competence, and "comfort in our skin," to name a few. The experience of many of these gifts increases with age (see Appendix 2). We cultivate wisdom and self-awareness through unpacking life's teachings. We become more resilient by going through our rough patches, which then equips and prepares us for the next difficulty. And we have earned greater competence and confidence as a function of experience within our professional and personal worlds.

We have earned these gifts; they are as much a part of our being as are our challenges. Acknowledging our gifts is an essential practice in order to feel the fullness of our lives. My hope is that you will more frequently notice, savor, and appreciate yours. One concrete way to do this is to apply SOFTT to your gifts.

Chapter 8

Applying Softt to the Gifts

"The more you praise and celebrate your life, the more there is in life to celebrate."

—Oprah

Toni is standing tall in the center of the yurt, directly below the "celestial crown" (a fitting term for the apex of the roof and of this moment). The sun shines through the crown like a spotlight on Toni and visible tree tops appear to stand ready to receive her words. It is the closing ceremony of an intensive workshop I am facilitating, called "A Day of Embracing the Middle," when participants share proud moments or accomplishments.

Toni's soft voice naturally amplifies in this spot: "I don't like coming to things like this alone. I am scared of what might come up for me, of being exposed, of not being in control. Coming with a friend is like a safety net, but none of mine were free, and that was ultimately a good thing. This is exactly what I needed, what I was craving. I am so grateful to be here, to have met you all, and I'm proud of myself for not caving in to fear. I didn't just show up alone...I *really* showed up!" The rest of us respond "Aho!" (a Native American word used for yes, I agree, or amen) in unison, as we witness and share in her proud moment.

Ellie steps up next. She looks up at the sky, opens her arms widely, and says, "I got my doctorate in Holistic Medicine last year and have felt like a fraud ever since. I am clear about what I have accomplished, and how hard I worked, but it still does not feel like me. I struggle with catching up with myself. I feel vulnerable saying this out loud but it is also liberating. I am not a fraud. I *am* a doctor. And, a damn good one." "Aho!" we cheer again.

One by one, each woman in the group takes her turn while the rest of us listen intently. It is a courageous moment for the women speaking and a beautiful sight to behold for the witnesses.

I always end these workshops with a practice of self-acknowledgement because most of us seldom go there. We tend to be proficient at self-criticism and can all too easily detail the ways we "could have" or "should have" done things differently. But few of us fully own our successes, simmer in their arrival, and appreciate the time and effort it took to achieve them.

How often have you told yourself, "I'm proud of myself for _____!" or "I'm a damn good ____!" when you earned it? If you are like most, the response is "rarely" or "never."

The same holds true for receiving praise. Rather than smile, say thank you, and enjoy a compliment, the more common response is a version of "Yes, but..." deflection, minimization, or diminishment, such as this exchange:

Colleague: "Great job!"
Presenter: "Really? I wasn't sure. I thought my closing was a bit rocky."
Colleague: "Nah, you nailed it."

Presenter: "Maybe, but it wasn't succinct. I need to make it more compelling."

Colleague: "It was very compelling. You were articulate and relatable. You answered their questions with finesse, except," she chuckles, "for that one long-winded woman."

Presenter: "Thanks—and crap, that woman! I knew I should have cut her off sooner. I have to get better at that."

Can you relate? I can. In fact, that was my exchange shortly after presenting at a conference where I received rave reviews and excellent evaluations. I could not fully see, much less receive, how well I did, nor could I fully enjoy the afterglow of a great presentation. Instead, my focus on my perceived shortcomings rapidly deflated my accomplishment, and myself, in the process. Bummer for me.

Perhaps you recognize similar patterns in yourself. Most of us can. This human inclination to see the downside of things is so common that there is a psychological term for it: negativity bias. In fact, not only do we focus on the negative more readily, but we also stay focused on these thoughts and reactions for longer periods than we do positive ones.

Rick Hanson colorfully captured this tendency in his book *Hardwiring Happiness* when he wrote: "Your brain is like Velcro for negative experiences but Teflon for positive ones." He further contends that this bias increases the negative (we over-react to negative situations, which stores them in our memory and increases stress, frustration, etc.) and reduces the positive (we underreact to the good situations, which makes them less likely to store in our memory bank).[18]

Our lives are full of positive shifts and experiences that merit our attention and celebration. We deserve to savor the good stuff and

---

[18]   Hanson, R. *Hardwiring Happiness: The New Brain Science of Contentment, Calm, and Happiness*. Harmony, 2013.

celebrate our accomplishments, at least as much as we feel the need to dwell on our challenges and shortcomings. The more we focus on our gifts and claim our accomplishments the more we can experience the joy and beauty in our lives and the bigger world. SOFTT provides a path to do just that.

Resistance of SOFTT to Gifts

In my daylong workshops, when I introduce the practice of SOFTT toward our gifts, there are always a few women who balk at the exercise. They have no qualms about using SOFTT with their hardships, but when I shift the focus to their achievements, several resist.

Some question the value or point, while others look visibly uncomfortable. "I can't think of anything," "This feels awkward," or "I don't know how" are common reactions. These women's resistance precisely highlights the need for dedicated attention and structure in this realm.

There are several reasons why it can be difficult for some people (particularly women) to own our achievements. This is true even when that ownership is purely an internal acknowledgment of something positive.

Social Conditioning

Social conditioning is one factor. Our awards and accomplishments are too often muted by societal expectations to be sensitive about how our successes can make others feel. The result is that we minimize or hide our accomplishments and, in some cases, even feel guilty about them. What!? How did *we* end up feeling badly about *our* earned feats? Unless it is an outright competition, *our success is not another person's failure.* It is our success.

Over time, many of us learned that there are also societal gender role assumptions and stereotypes concerning what is considered appropriate behavior for women. Self-praise is not one of them. Humility and modesty are lauded far more than pride. As a result, many of us shy away from fully recognizing our accomplishments, and our power, for fear of being perceived as bragging.

This social conditioning is baked into our language, as dictionaries plainly demonstrate. Synonyms for self-praise include arrogance, boastfulness, bragging, conceit, egoism, immodesty, narcissism, pride, self-absorption, self-admiration, self-aggrandizement. Wow! Aside from pride, these terms are all pejorative and clearly imply that standing tall and owning our successes is bad.

To be clear, I am not advocating that we brag or boast. Rather, I invite us to fully own our gifts and successes, to name and claim what we have earned, and to give ourselves the acknowledgment we deserve. Whether we applaud ourselves internally or share our success with a friend, it is for us; it is not for, or at the expense of, anyone else.

Self-Doubt

Another adversary to self-praise is self-doubt. We may doubt the value of our accomplishments because they did not reach unrealistically high standards or because we think they pale in comparison to someone else's. Most of us have experienced the well-known imposter phenomenon, where we feel fraudulent and unworthy of our accolades despite evidence demonstrating our competence. The authors of the founding study[19] around the imposter experience actually coined the term "imposter *phenomenon*" because it is such a common experience.

---

[19] Clance, PR and Imes, SA. (Fall, 1978). *The Impostor Phenomenon in High Achieving Women: Dynamics and Therapeutic Intervention. Psychotherapy:* Theory, Research, & Practice. 15(3): 241-247

Over time, it morphed into "imposter *syndrome*," a change that pathologized a very normal experience, especially among women.

Self-doubt and diminishing conditioned responses to successes are powerful forces that most of us will face at some point in our lives. But when we succumb to them as a pattern, we keep ourselves small and feel disempowered. We diminish our successes, and ourselves, in the process. When we stand tall and own our big and small wins, we not only reinforce our worthiness and power but can also help others see and claim theirs.

Definition of Accomplishment

What are your criteria for an accomplishment? Does it require a form of external validation, such as a promotion, an award, or a professional certification? Does it need to be visible or meaningful to others? Must it be perfect to be worthy of acknowledgment? Many of us have limiting criteria, mostly unexamined, for determining what constitutes a success.

One of my greatest accomplishments of 2023 was to convince my in-laws to receive necessary aid from a part-time caregiver. Not only was it best for them, but it also met my need to establish boundaries. This was a years-long effort and when they finally agreed, I was elated, relieved, and proud. Carla's success was to turn down a board position in order to prioritize self-care and Keshia's was to join a board, despite her fear of having nothing to offer. None of these successes came with a certificate, trophy, or degree and they were all worthy of celebration.

We can also easily overlook the smaller, daily feats that are personally significant, those mundane actions or experiences that make a positive impact on our lives. I am not particularly adept at cooking or dressing fashionably. When I prepare a tasty meal or pull together a cute outfit, I am thrilled. For others, a mundane success could be going to sleep earlier, being patient with a trying family member, or relegating a house chore to someone else.

> The most important measure of an accomplishment is that it *positively impacts your life, or those people, values, or organizations that you treasure.* A desire and intentional effort are all that's required. Perfectionism is optional. The implicit award is an easier, more satisfying life.

Self-praise is a physically and emotionally healthy practice. It feels good, is empowering, and can offset the negativity bias. When you take a few minutes to apply SOFTT to your successes, it will help train your mind to increasingly notice and appreciate the frequency of positive moments and experiences in your life.

Let's give it a shot. First, choose a recent accomplishment. It need not be anything profound. List options. You can either:

1) Close your eyes and allow an accomplishment to come into your consciousness, without overthinking the criteria,

2) Say to yourself, "I'm proud of_____," and notice what arises, or

3) Scan the chart on the next few pages to jolt your memory.

Personal Development	**Educational Achievements:** ❋ Completing a degree or certification program ❋ Acquiring new skills through workshops, courses, or self-study
	Physical and Mental Wellness: ❋ Less concern about what others think ❋ More confidence ❋ More "comfort in your skin" ❋ A healthier lifestyle, better diet, or achieving an exercise goal ❋ Not "sweating the small stuff" ❋ Advocating for your needs ❋ Prioritizing self-care
	Relationships: ❋ Less people-pleasing ❋ Better boundaries ❋ Successfully navigating challenges in a relationship ❋ Building and maintaining meaningful friendships ❋ Launching your kids ❋ Managing caretaking of elders ❋ Celebrating a milestone anniversary with a partner
Professional Accomplishments	**Career Advancements:** ❋ A promotion or a higher position at work ❋ Successfully leading a team or project to completion ❋ Expanding your professional network and establishing valuable connections
	Project Success: ❋ Completing a significant project ❋ Receiving positive feedback or recognition for a job well done ❋ Contributing to a project that has a positive impact on the organization
	Skills Development: ❋ More competence in an existing skill ❋ Learning a new skill relevant to your profession ❋ Successfully implementing new technologies or processes ❋ Completing professional certifications or training programs

Personal Achievements	**Hobbies and Interests:** ✳ Taking up a new hobby or interest ✳ Persevering on a challenging creative project, such as writing a book or another type of artistic endeavor ✳ Successfully organizing or participating in an event related to your passion **Volunteer and Community Work:** ✳ Making a positive impact through volunteering or community service ✳ Leading a community initiative or project ✳ Receiving recognition for contributions to a charitable cause **Financial Accomplishments:** ✳ Meeting savings or investment goals ✳ Successfully budgeting and achieving financial stability ✳ Paying off significant debts
Personal Growth	**Overcoming Personal Challenges:** ✳ Stepping out of your comfort zone ✳ Successfully navigating a major life transition ✳ Bouncing back from challenges more easily (i.e., resilience) ✳ Greater self-awareness of limiting beliefs and patterns **Cultural and Travel Experiences:** ✳ Learning a new language or immersing yourself in a new culture ✳ Traveling to new places and experiencing personal growth through exploration ✳ Successfully planning and executing a memorable trip **Spiritual Development:** ✳ Achieving personal milestones in your spiritual or religious journey ✳ Exploring meditation or mindfulness ✳ Incorporating spiritual practices into your daily life ✳ More faith or trust

Set-Up. Having selected one accomplishment on which to fully focus, consider its evolution from inception to completion. Reflect on the work it took, and recall the hurdles you overcame to achieve it. Do not minimize your efforts or obstacles. Picture, imagine, or feel this accomplishment in its fullness. Then you are ready for Step 1.

Step 1 – Slow Down and Breathe. Close your eyes and take at least three slow, deep, and deliberate breaths. Allow your mind and body to settle. Relax into a natural rate and rhythm of breathing. When you are ready, proceed to Step 2.

Step 2 – Observe Your Thoughts and Emotions. Gently observe and then gently release any thoughts and emotions associated with your success. Allow them all to flow without restraint, judgment, or engagement, even if they seem contradictory. Take your time.

Consider the following possible thoughts that may arise when we open up to our successes:

* I'm proud!
* This was a big deal!
* It wasn't that big of a deal—anyone could do it.
* I don't give myself enough credit.
* Yay, me!
* It's about time.

Feelings associated with an accomplishment can include:

* Excitement
* Embarrassment

* Fear
* Disappointment
* Pressure
* Pride

Once you have observed and released your thoughts and emotions, move to Step 3.

Step 3 – Feel the Physical Sensations Practice a body scan (discussed in Chapter 6) to hone in on your physical sensations.

Do you feel buzzing energy and if so, where?
Is there a lightness or tightness?
Do you feel calm, expansive, or restricted?
What is happening in your eyes, jaws, neck?

Once you have connected with your body, move to Step 4.

Step 4 – Apply Tenderness. Give yourself celebratory tenderness. Rather than place your hand on your heart, consider patting yourself on the back, or giving yourself a congratulatory hug. Use tender words such as "Well done!" "Yay, me!" or "This was a big deal!" If words escape you, imagine what you would say to a friend who had achieved something personally noteworthy.

Do not rush this part. Feel it and enjoy it for as long as you like. If you are uncomfortable giving yourself tender recognition, return to Steps 2 and 3: observe your thoughts and emotions and feel your bodily sensations. Then try the tenderness step again.

Step 5 – Tune In To Your Inner Wisdom. Does your inner teacher have any insights or reminders for you about your accomplishments? Feel into the answer, and allow whatever is within you to arise.

Does it feel good to give yourself praise?
Do you feel unworthy of your own praise?
Do you tend to diminish your accomplishments?
What did you learn from this accomplishment to carry forward?

Wrap-Up. What was it like to give yourself some well-deserved acknowledgment? What did you learn from practicing SOFTT with a success? If the process was uncomfortable, difficult, or awkward, that's okay. For many, this is new territory. Try SOFTT another time, with a different success. For a more powerful experience, apply SOFTT to an accomplishment or proud moment when it has just occurred. You deserve it!

Conclusion

In February 2024, I watched Niecy Nash-Betts' emotional acceptance speech for winning an Emmy for Outstanding Supporting Actress. As she received the trophy, she proudly raised it to the sky and yelled, "I'm a winner, baby!" Niecy proceeded to thank several of the usual people before giving a loud shout-out to a rarely recognized person:

> And you know who else I wanna thank? I wanna thank me, for believing in me and doing what they said I could not do. And I wanna say to myself in front of all you beautiful people, "Go on, girl, with your bad self!"[20]

---

[20]   Primetime Emmy Awards, January 2024, CBS Television Network

I hooted for Niecy in my living room. It was not only what Niecy said but *how* she said it. She stood tall, looked directly at the audience, and praised herself with full, unapologetic passion. And the audience loved it! That's what I'm talking about.

The Bottom Line

SOFTT helps us to see and experience the fullness of our midlife evolution by celebrating our accomplishments, no matter how large or small. When we only focus on our challenges, we shortchange our efforts and can cultivate a narrow, depressing, and disempowering life narrative and experience. Our efforts, our hard-earned gifts, deserve to be celebrated. We own them. We are them. When we regularly apply SOFTT to our successes and growth, we establish a new pattern, one where we remain mindful of their presence and can start to naturally and more consistently become more aware of them in our daily lives. And that is a beautiful sight to behold in ourselves.

At the end of the book is a bookmark you can use as a handy reference for SOFTT.

PART 3

CHANGING THE MIDLIFE PARADIGM

CHAPTER 9

THE "ANDS" OF MIDLIFE

"The cultivation of joyfulness teaches us a great deal about coexistence. Yes, there is affliction, there is that which is broken, there is that which is heartbreaking in life; and it lives side by side with that which is well, that which can be celebrated, that which can be appreciated."

—Jaya Rudgard

I vividly remember a student-teacher conversation I had many years back with my Zen teacher, Diane. I was grappling with an ancient issue around body image and frustrated that it had reared its head again. I thought I was done.

As Diane and I talk only intermittently, I also shared other things going on for me: gratitude for a spiritual practice, pride in my daughters' evolutions, excitement about my research, and my issue. That stinking issue.

"I'd like to call your attention to the word 'and,'" was Diane's response to my five-minute rant.

"What word?" I asked, thinking I misheard her.

"The word 'and,'" she repeated.

Diane then reflected my monologue back to me with amazing detail. She reminded me that I started our conversation by mentioning gratitude. I then shared my feelings of frustration, pride, and aliveness. She emphasized that although that old issue was back again, it was part of the vastness of my current experience. It was an "and" perched between gratitude and aliveness. Diane reminded me that my delights and frustrations are not disconnected parts of my life; they are all my life. This beautiful, yet simple teaching was profoundly impactful and helped me to appreciate the many concurrent experiences happening in my world rather than define it only by my challenge.

Midlife is a season of "ands." Our eyesight is waning at the same time we "see" things with more clarity. Our wombs are closing as our freedom to explore midlife callings is simultaneously opening. Our loved ones are undeniably fading as our sense of personal choice and agency are alive and growing. And despite our bounty of wrinkle creams, we are still "more comfortable in our skin." To me, the many "ands" are part of what makes midlife so rich in opportunity and growth.

A big focus of "embracing the middle" is to bring awareness to our "ands"—to widen our inner and outer lens in order to be more present to the entire tapestry. At my Embrace the Middle workshops, I always ask the participants to bring symbols or objects that represent significant features of their current midlife experience. I do not provide examples of what to bring because I don't want to influence their choices. As women enter the yurt, where I hold my events, they place their symbols on a designated midlife altar.

The first time I asked participants to bring symbolic objects to a workshop, I hoped that the exercise would not backfire. I wondered if our altar would look like a drug store, full of wrinkle creams and supplements. True to my concern, participants' initial instinct was to bring items in those categories, namely reading glasses and sleep aids. But, or rather *and*, the majority also brought symbols that reflected their midlife accomplishments or shifts—their "ands." This continues to be the case at every workshop.

Over the years, the symbols have clustered into one of three categories. Here are a few examples:

* **Representations of physical aging:** anti-aging products, balms for sore muscles, handheld fans, glasses, a knee brace, medications, hormone creams, walking sticks, a "breast cancer survivor" sign, and always sleep aids (be it melatonin, essential oils, or CBD gummies). One woman placed her favorite lubricant—coconut oil—on the altar.

* **Symbols of midlife accomplishments:** certificates and diplomas, new business cards, an owl candle (reflecting one's wisdom), a marathon finisher medal, a discarded bottle of root cover-up, artwork, and even a crown from one woman's fifth decade "queenhood" party.

* **Symbols of midlife intentions:** passports and "road trip" music, a ceramic heart with an open hand reflecting an attendee's efforts to be more "open-hearted," a packet of seeds which capture another's new beginning. One attendee brought her scale, which she wanted to release. After the workshop, we supported and cheered her on as she threw the scale into a trash can.

I love these altars and how beautifully and visually they capture the many "ands" of midlife. We are validated and moved when we learn about each other's choices of symbols and the stories behind them. Not only can we empathize with the shared challenges but we often get helpful tips for better sleep, menopausal symptom relief, and self-care. And, it is a delight when we share and listen to each other's achievements and aspirations.

"Ands" and Grief

For me, the concept of "ands" was an invaluable tool during my grief journeys. A few of my "and" mourning moments are etched in my memory. One was the last morning of my mother's shiva, the Jewish seven-day mourning period, when it is customary to take a closing walk. I recall opening the door of my childhood home for our rabbi, who came to lead us on the ritual walk. My dad, heavy from grief, stood up slowly to join the rabbi, followed by my dad's dog Aimee, me, and my nephew Ben. Together, we stepped into the blazing heat and humidity of New Orleans. I held my dad's arm to steady him as we walked in silence for fifteen minutes, at which time our rabbi signaled for us to stop. The four of us (and Aimee, whom I am convinced joined us in the ritual) stood in a circle. Rabbi Greenberg then said something like this:

> We are now concluding shiva, which is the deepest, hardest part of the grief and healing journey. For seven days, your job has only been to mourn, nothing else. Per the ritual, you were instructed to not leave your home unless to go to synagogue, nor to look in mirrors, or even stand up for guests. You have only grieved. Now it is time to slowly emerge from the disorientation and singularity of your sorrow. Take a look around and notice the sky and trees, the world around you. Your grief is still profound but there is also life around you.

To me, or perhaps from my life lens, Rabbi Greenberg was introducing "ands" into our grief. He did not say our mourning was over. We were far from that. His guidance, the guidance of shiva, was to continue to grieve *and* to be mindful of other aspects of life, even if just the blue sky. It was a profound moment for me.

Remembering "ands" continued to help me during subsequent periods of mourning, especially after Eddie passed. When overcome with sorrow, I would often take long hikes up a nearby mountain. During one of these hikes, as tears streamed down my cheeks, I was "awakened" from a haze of sorrow by a breeze on my face. The crisp air cooled my cheeks and dried my tears. I paused to take in the sun and allow its rays to warm my damp skin. Then I noticed magnificent clouds, which I had been entirely oblivious to throughout the hike. I was hurting *and* could appreciate and enjoy my beautiful surroundings. Opening up to the fullness of nature soothed me and reminded me that my life was much bigger than my sorrow. It was another profound moment of "ands."

Awareness of "Ands" as a Meditation Practice

During my weekly meditation groups, I sometimes use the practice of "ands" as our focus. I guide the participants to expand their awareness from their breath to the many "ands" in their environment. Rather than explain how I do this, here is an example.

I encourage you to try the practice, rather than only read about it, as the experience of "ands" is much more compelling than its description. You can either have a friend read the directions aloud while you practice or listen to its recording on my Embrace the Middle website.

Set-Up

Find a quiet place to sit, with minimal distractions. Put your phone in a different room. If you must have it near you, place it upside down, on silent mode. If there are other people around you, request that they keep their voices down and close any doors to limit distracting sounds.

The Practice

1. Sit in an upright position, on a cushion on the floor, or in a chair. (Lying down is not recommended as that signals your body to rest and can decrease your attention.) Make sure your posture is tall and alert since the goal is to widen our attention. This is similar to when our parents or teachers used to say, "Sit up straight and pay attention." Your hands can rest comfortably in your lap.

2. Close your eyes or lower your gaze to minimize visual distractions.

3. To begin, take a few slower, deeper breaths, similar to Step 1 of the SOFTT practice. Breathe in, from the diaphragm, for a count of three to five seconds, and exhale for a few seconds longer. Make sure you fully exhale. The counting of the inbreath and outbreath can anchor your attention. Take at least three of these intentionally slower breaths and then relax into a comfortable, natural rhythm of breathing.

4. Notice any sensations around your bottom where it touches the chair, couch or cushion. Feel any sensations in your feet, and where they connect with the floor or cushion. Feel your hands resting in your lap.

5. Bring your attention to the center of your chest, and notice how your chest rises and falls with your breath. If it helps, place your hand on your chest to feel its expansion on the inhale and deflation on the exhale. Stay here for at least five rounds of this intentional breathing, just being aware of the movement of the chest, with the breath.

6. If and when thoughts arise, which almost always happens, just imagine them drifting along like a cloud in the sky, and return your attention to the rising and falling of your chest, with your breath. You may have to do this several times throughout the meditation. That is normal.

7. Now, try to expand your attention from your chest and breath to include any sounds in your environment. You may hear the whirring of electronics, voices in another room, birds chirping, or cars passing by. Avoid labeling them as good or bad, pleasant or unpleasant. Just notice the sounds and your breath, which are coexisting. They are "ands." Stay here for several rounds of your breath.

8. Next, while still being mindful of your chest and breath, become aware of the temperature in the room. If you are breathing through your nose, notice that the air is cooler on the inhalation, and warmer on the exhalation. Perhaps your feet and hands are chilly or warm, while other parts of your body are less sensitive to the temperature. The temperature is an "and" with your breath. Stay here for a few more rounds of breath.

9. Choose the easiest "and" or "ands"—sounds, temperature, or awareness of differing bodily sensations—to add to your breath. Stay here for a few minutes, in this more expansive state of awareness. When you are ready, open your eyes.

As you transition back to your day or night, choose an "and" to accompany your activities. While on your computer, notice your breath between answering emails. When you walk to your car, pause and look at the sky. If you are washing dishes, feel the sensation of the water on your fingers. These are all "ands."

Set an intention to remain mindful of your co-occurring "ands." Awareness of "ands" reminds us that our lives are not limited to the immediacy of our thoughts, feelings, or external activities. There is always a larger container within which these occur.

As a concrete reminder, create your own altar to remind yourself of the many "ands" alive in your life. The possibilities of "ands" are personal and unlimited. They could include pictures, items from nature, or a religious/spiritual symbol. When you pass your altar, pause to take it all in, and bow in recognition and honor of the many "ands" that are part of your midlife reality.

Creating Your Own Altar

1. Find a special, private space where your altar can stay intact. It is for you, not your friends or family.

2. Designate and adorn your altar surface. It could be a small end table, top of a box, or even a section on a floor. If the surface itself is not aesthetically appealing, paint it, lay down a colorful scarf, or choose bright objects to enhance its appeal. (I always have a fresh flower and candle on mine, which I light when I meditate nearby.)

3. Choose objects that reflect your midlife reality, desired state, or aspirations: crystals, pictures of loved ones alive or passed, flowers, symbols of a goal—it only has to be meaningful to you.

4. Update your altar as you evolve. When a symbol no longer applies, thank it and remove it. Replace it if, and only if, there is another meaningful symbol. If nothing fits in the moment, honor the space, and be open to what may arrive.

The Bottom Line

Every moment of our lives is awash in "ands." Regardless of what is going on, it is always accompanied by the beauty of sunrises and sunsets, the sounds of birds or airplanes overhead, and the beating of our hearts. These are small reminders of the vastness of our lives, the constant presence of challenges and gifts.

It can be easy, however, to lose sight of the positive, or even neutral, "ands." When the challenges consume the lion's share of our time and attention, we can become negatively myopic in our focus and thoughts.

Opening up to the "ands" reminds us that life is more than any singular event or struggle; it is an intentional practice of being mindful of the array of things that always coexist. Awareness of the "ands" can provide more space around the difficulties and bring more joy into our lives. These many "ands" are not merely disparate parts of a tapestry of existence—they are the tapestry. Notice them, embrace them, and feel the difference, even if just for a few seconds.

CHAPTER 10

OUR COLLECTIVE WISDOM

*"Women's strength, women's industry, women's wisdom
are humankind's greatest untapped resource."*

—Michelle Bachelet

When my oldest daughter was three, I bought a book called *My Grand-mother's Story*. It consists of simple questions, which my daughters could ask my mom (Bubbe) to get to know her better. "What were you like when you were young?" "Did you have any hobbies?" "What was your favorite subject in school?" are a few examples. Whenever my parents visited us in California, I brought out the book. And, every time I flew to New Orleans, or met my parents somewhere else, I packed that book—it took no fewer than fifty trips to New Orleans and accompanied me to dozens of family get-togethers around the country. Sometimes it would stay in my suitcase, while other times it would get unpacked yet lay around unopened. But it was always there.

My daughters and I (I took over interviewing when they grew weary of it) did not ask the questions in order. We would flip through the book and choose a topic that interested us in the moment. Since we completed the book over the course of fifteen years, it includes my daughters' youthful block letters, misspelled words, and funny commentary, like "Bad girl, Bubbe" (for the time she blamed her sister for finishing an apple pie) or "You were silly" (when she said she was proud that she broke her nose playing softball because she caught a fastball). I love those! There are also answers in both my mom's distinctive cursive and my own messy handwriting.

The last time any of us wrote in the book was April 2018. The occasion was in Dallas, where several family members convened to attend a gala that my brother and sister-and-law chaired. Because my parents were coming, the book came along, too. The afternoon before the event, my mom, now in the early stages of dementia, was sitting at my brother's kitchen table. I sat down next to her, book in hand. "Let's see what's left, Mom," I said. As was typical, I started flipping through the book, looking for a blank page. Lo and behold, the only page not completed was the very last one. And here was the question:

Me (reading the question to my mom): "Grandma, do you have any advice for me?"

My mom (after pausing for a second): "Was I a good mom?"

Me: "Of course you were and still are a good mom, but that's not the question. The question is do you have any advice for your grandchildren?" By this time, my two daughters, two nieces, and nephew were gathered around the table.

My mom (looking around the table): "Was I a good grandmother?" The kids collectively chimed in, "You're the best, Bubbe," "Of course you are," and "We love you, Bubbe." I tried one last time, repeating the question. My mom again responded with a question, this time asking if she was a good role model for her children.

By now, fourteen of us, including my dad, were seated or standing around the table. I closed the book and said, "Okay, everyone. Since so many of us are here together, we're going to give Mom an early Mother's Day present. Let's go around the table and answer Mom's questions about whether she is a good mom, grandmother, and role model."

One by one, over the course of an hour, we went around the table, individually answering the myriad ways she was a wonderful mom, bubbe, and role model. We laughed and were teary eyed at everyone's touching answers and the many different ways she was beyond good in all of those roles. It was a beautiful, moving experience and one of the last gifts she would receive. My mom died six weeks later.

I do not know if my mom unconsciously, or perhaps consciously, knew that she was approaching the end. She was not physically sick, in any apparent way, at the time. But clearly, the answers to her direct, pressing questions were foremost on her mind. To me, my mom's questions illustrated her advice, her wisdom, not only to her grandchildren but to all of us sitting there that day: Be a good mother/father. Be a good grandmother/grandfather. Be a good role model.

During the interviews for my research, the final question I asked was a version of that last question in *My Grandmother's Story* book. It was:

What wisdom would you impart to others from your midlife lens?

The rest of this chapter is a summary of the interviewees' responses. Some of their wisdom is concrete ("Stay the course") and some existential ("Find out who you are distinct from mom, daughter, and wife"). Some pertain to how we treat ourselves ("Trust yourself") and some to how we treat others ("Appreciate that your parents did the best they could"). Their generous teachings are not intellectual cliches or aspirations; they are embodied wisdom accrued along these women's individual journeys.

Before I share their responses, reflect on your own guiding wisdom. What sage advice, from this period of your life, would *you* impart to others? For some of you, wisdom may pour forth like water from a fountain. One that immediately comes to mind for me is "We all do the best we can, with the resources we have, at each point in our lives." When I ruminate on past relationships, disappointments, or regrets, I find comfort in this wisdom. It helped me to release anger and heal longstanding issues with key people in my life.

If your advice is not evident, try writing a letter to your younger self. Choose a decade in which you struggled and then offer wisdom from your current perspective. Perhaps it could start "Dear twenty-five-year-old-self, I want you to know that..." Alternatively, consider what you would advise a room of thirty-year-olds who are curious to know what you learned in later decades. You may be surprised at how much wisdom, how much sage advice, you have to offer.

The categories below include the most frequently cited wisdom relayed by the interviewees. The bulleted comments are the women's verbatim responses. I am certain that you will connect with many—and have equally valuable wisdom to add.

May you find validation, comfort, and guidance from this collection of midlife women's words of wisdom.

On Authenticity

* Be authentic; it's like coming home to yourself.
* Do you! Be you! You cannot rush what it's not yet time for.
* Show up regardless of what you're feeling.
* Enjoy life. Don't feel guilty about doing what you love.
* Be true to yourself, not to what others want you to be or do.

On Decision and Regrets

* Listen for a "Full Body Yes."
* It's okay to change your mind; circumstances change all the time.
* Don't let past decisions puncture a hole in future decisions.
* Don't look back with regret; the decision was right at that point in time.
* Make peace with your past. Look forward, not backward.
* Think before acting.

On Self-Doubt

* You are so much stronger than you realize.
* Take risks and trust your ability to do them.
* Go for it! Drop "should" and follow your heart.
* Go inside; your body will tell you if something is working for you or not.
* Stand head to toe with fear and ask yourself, "What is the worst thing that could happen?"

On Relationships

* Life is not about things; it's about relationships and experiences.
* Make your partner and relationships a priority.
* Your parents and kids won't always be around. Enjoy your time with them while you can.
* Appreciate that your parents did the best they could; we all make parenting mistakes.
* Don't give up on your children; stay the course.

* Have low expectations of others. It will contribute to your happiness.
* Build a nice circle, a tribe, who you "get" and who really "gets" you.
* Be open to older mentors or role models; they are awesome in this stage of life.
* Surround yourself with people who lift you up.
* Be of service to others. It's a tremendous source of fulfillment.
* Give freely, without expectation of getting anything back.
* Love generously; there is no sacrifice in love.

On Growth

* Slow down and enjoy the journey.
* There is only one place you are going on your journey and that is home to yourself.
* Consider what would matter most when you look back on your life.
* Step out of your comfort zone. If you are scared, do it anyway.
* Say "yes" to everything for twenty-four hours.
* Ask yourself, "What can I experience now that I can't in the future?" Once it's passed, the gold is harvested.
* Only the present moment contains life. Be engaged with who you are in this moment.
* Discover who you are apart from mom, wife, and daughter.
* Don't be afraid of aging. Each stage brings wonderful gifts.
* Your challenges are part of you and make you a complete person. We are bred from how we handle them.
* Your superpowers are born from your wounds.

✴ Believe in magical possibilities; we live in a rich and mysterious world with endless possibilities and opportunities.

On Self-Acceptance

✴ Spend more time being okay with you.

✴ Replace perfectionism with self-compassion. It feels much better.

✴ Even in your imperfections, you are perfect; there's a divinity in that we are always evolving.

✴ Be kind to yourself.

✴ Don't take yourself so seriously.

✴ Acknowledge and accept wherever you are.

On Self-Care

✴ Nurture your own needs first. It helps everyone.

✴ Put to bed the word "should." It never brings up good feelings.

✴ Advocate for yourself. You are the best one for the job.

✴ You don't have to suffer from menopause.

✴ Ask for help when you need it; it takes strength.

✴ Be in the driver's seat, not the passenger's, in your journey through life.

The Bottom Line

We have a wealth of individual wisdom from our unique life experiences, and our midlife, collective, female wisdom is boundless. We can be inspired by our midlife sisters' experiences and lessons about themselves, their relationships with others, and their guiding principles. It has served them and may serve you as well. Draw on the wisdom of others, as they can from yours, for guidance, validation, and aspiration.

In the final chapter, we explore the power of the collective by discussing ways we can begin to challenge and change the midlife paradigm and the ways many of us are negatively treated.

CHAPTER 11

HOW TO CHANGE THE PARADIGM

"We need women at all levels, including the top, to change the dynamic, reshape the conversation, to make sure women's voices are heard and heeded, not overlooked and ignored."

—Sheryl Sandberg

On our journey throughout this book, I have emphasized the power of our individual choice to embrace, rather than deny or reject, mid-life. And, it is critical to acknowledge that we live within a social and cultural context, that is bigger than the individual. We cannot choose the culture within which we live. The midlife climate, as illustrated in this book, can be unkind. Many of the ingrained beliefs pertaining to women in this stage, and the negative ways we may be treated, have deep historical, cultural, and societal roots. Patriarchal systems, where men held the power and privilege, have a long history, as does the societal emphasis on women's beauty.

Thanks to feminist champions and initiatives, movements such as #metoo, increased menopause support, and advocates for gender equality, women have made significant headway in changing these long-standing patterns. And there is more to be done. Far too often, women continue to be relegated to the sidelines simply due to the fact that we have been alive for forty plus years.

Change in these realms starts at home. Naturally, as we awaken to our gifts and power, we become less tolerant of this harsh midlife environment. I invite us to apply our wisdom and self-awareness to the world we live in by challenging disempowering patterns. When we reject menopausal secrecy, workplace dismissal, and youthful standards of beauty, we collectively loosen their roots.

Our efforts can support one another, even as they serve our daughters, granddaughters, nieces, younger colleagues, and future generations. Together, we can refute and stop these patterns from being perpetuated. To this end, I offer a few examples of ways we can collaboratively begin to alter the midlife climate for the better.

Menopause

In May 2024, *Ms. Magazine* published an article titled "Menopause is Fueling a Movement: A New Generation of Women are Demanding that the Next Chapter of their Lives No Longer Be Ignored, Overlooked or Squandered." Indeed, in recent years, there has been an explosion of publications, advocacy, personal storytelling, legislation, conferences, and grassroots efforts centered on the topic of menopause. There is even now a World Menopause Day on October 18.

A number of high-profile female leaders and celebrities, including Halle Berry, Michelle Obama, Tracee Ellis Ross, Maria Shriver, and Oprah Winfrey publicly discuss menopause, host women's summits, and advocate for positive aging. Tamsen Fadal, a former journalist, author, and now menopause advocate with a tremendous following, hosts #MenopauseTok—a week-long virtual gathering of education and inspiration for menopausal women. She, along with Denise

Pines, founder of WisePause Wellness, came together to produce an upcoming PBS documentary called *The M Factor: Shredding the Silence on Menopause*.

There are a growing number of impressive bloggers on *Substack* who write about perimenopause and menopause, and podcasters who discuss specific aspects of menopause, including well-researched scientific information on hormone replacement therapy and previously unimaginable, intimate conversations focusing on the sexual challenges of menopause.

I am deeply grateful for all of these women and initiatives. And we need to do our part.

Here are some ways:

Let's Talk about Menopause

Literally, let's talk about it. The majority of women I interviewed never discussed hormonal changes and challenges with their mothers. Our mother's generation did not openly have these conversations because it violated their cultural norms; they believed it was a private experience, shrouded in secrecy. My mother and I could barely get through the "birds and bees" conversation, much less menopause, even though she had an emergency hysterectomy after giving birth to my youngest brother. In fact, I had never even heard of the term perimenopause until my symptoms caused me to seek help.

Our mothers' menopausal silence did not serve us—many of us were caught off guard and felt confused when we found ourselves in its midst, experiencing unexpected symptoms and changes. We were relieved and felt normal when we learned that our girlfriends had similar challenges. However, we would have been much more relaxed had we known these were common symptoms, rather than wondering if something was wrong with us. If we perpetuate the silence around menopause, we are perpetuating our experience, and not helping future generations of women to be more informed and prepared for these changes and to understand the options to reduce their distress.

Fortunately, the current cultural climate is shifting toward a greater vocalization and appreciation of menopause's complexity. Unlike our mothers, more and more women currently in midlife are comfortable having these conversations. More importantly, many *want* to have these conversations, and not just in hushed corners of our offices or exclusively with our girlfriends. Generation Xers, born between 1965 and 1980, not only more openly talk about their menopausal experiences but are also more comfortable asking for support than women in previous generations. Millennials, born between 1981 and 1996, in the age of the internet explosion, are information gatherers. I believe that they will want, if not demand, to know what lies ahead and will have little tolerance for avoidance of these conversations.

We can help propel this change by unapologetically and openly sharing our menopausal experiences. Use the courage and forthrightness of influential menopausal champions as your inspiration to talk freely about your menopausal realities. The more it is discussed, the less awkward it feels and the more informed everyone becomes.

Health-Care Providers

Many medical professionals, especially male doctors, are not extensively educated about menopause, nor do they all listen with compassionate ears to their patients. In one of Dr. Kelly Casperson's podcasts, *You are Not Broken*,[21] she explains that two decades of doctors were not trained about menopause, largely as a result of an extensive Women's Health Initiative study which claimed that hormone replacement therapy (HRT) causes breast cancer. The slated eight-year trial was

---

21   https://kellycaspersonmd.com/boomers-should-be-pissed/

designed to explore whether hormone therapy lowers the risk of heart disease. After five years, however, the study was abruptly and prematurely terminated when a study-monitoring group did not see the hoped for decline in heart disease and saw a slight risk of breast cancer. The latter finding was the bombshell takeaway. This resulted in an immediate and extensive cessation of HRT treatment, which was helping thousands and thousands of women (my own mother included.) Though the findings were questioned, especially given the older age of the participants, and subsequent research has demonstrated the numerous positive effects of hormone replacement, the damage took decades to undo and continues to influence some physicians' reluctance to prescribe hormones.

A second outcome of insufficient training is a tendency for some doctors to attribute menopausal symptoms to anxiety or stress, which is frustrating and diminishing to their patients. Leah said that she felt "broken," as a result of her male doctor minimizing and pathologizing her hormone-induced struggles. She wondered if she was the only one having this degree of hormone-related disruption in her life. It was only after doing her own research that she found validation, treatment options, and a new doctor.

Though menopause is happening concurrently with other challenging issues, and symptoms can have an array of causes, that does not preclude the hormonal relationship to many of them. It is imperative that our medical doctor more extensively understand and de-pathologize menopause. They must learn as much about the different treatment options for menopause as they do erectile dysfunction and Viagra. That would be a good start.

Fortunately, there are recent grassroots movements within the medical field to help spread this knowledge. One example is a group who call themselves "The Menoposse"—a coalition of currently more than 200 clinicians who share research, case studies, and best practices to support the treatment of their clients. Their mission is to "push boundaries, challenge the status quo, and use their voices to force a change in how women going through menopause are cared for."[22]

There are also initiatives on the federal level advocating for more research into women's unique health issues, including the impact of menopause on women's health and well-being.[23]

Despite these advances, we should not passively wait for more change to happen from within the medical field; we still need to speak up and advocate for our needs. Share all of your symptoms and ask for treatment guidance. If your physician is unable to provide this guidance, request a referral to a treatment provider more versed in menopause.

If you have a negative experience with a medical provider, and are able to address it directly in the moment, this self-advocacy increases momentum for change. I realize these are difficult conversations to initiate. An alternative option is to send a signed or anonymous letter to your doctor, in which you detail your experience and its impact. If you choose to change doctors because of frustration with their response to your menopausal challenges, inform them why you made this decision. It would be a service to them and their other patients who struggle with menopausal symptoms.

In the words of Maya Angelou, "Each time a woman stands up for herself, without knowing it possibly, without claiming it, she stands up for all women."

---

[22]   https://www.mariashriversundaypaper.com/
       dr-mary-claire-haver-new-menopause/

[23]   https://www.congress.gov/bill/118th-congress/house-bill/6749/text

Educate Yourself

For our own benefit, we should not exclusively rely on our medical providers or friends for menopause-related information. Along with our symptoms, women's treatment needs and preferences vary tremendously. Use the wealth of reliable, public information to educate yourself and address your unique needs.

There is an abundance of books on menopause, including these newer best sellers: *The New Menopause: Navigating Your Path Through Hormonal Change with Purpose, Power, and Facts* by Dr. Mary Claire Haver; *Grown Woman Talk: Your Guide to Getting and Staying Healthy* by Dr. Sharon Malone; and *The Menopause Brain: New Science Empowers Women to Navigate the Pivotal Transition with Knowledge and Confidence* by Dr. Lisa Mosconi.

There are also featured newspaper, journal, and magazine articles, podcasts, and websites specifically dedicated to menopause. As with any source of information, reliability is key; be discerning about where you get your information.

A good place to start is the North American Menopause Society, the International Menopause Society, and the National Menopause Foundation, whose websites include scientific based research and resources that are available to the public. These are just a few examples of the plethora of public information at our fingertips.

Men and Menopause

It is critical that men beyond the health-care field are included in conversations addressing the menopausal realities of their partners, friends, family members, and colleagues. Understanding fosters compassion and offers a starting point to minimize stigmatizing, stereotyping, and tasteless jokes at our expense.

Victoria, an interviewee, shared her experience of having severe, unpredictable hot flashes during meetings with her male colleagues. Not only was she embarrassed to drip in sweat midway through a meeting, but she also felt professionally diminished by the judgmental stares from her male colleagues. If her colleagues were informed and sensitive, she or they could suggest a five-minute break when they noticed her hot flash. This would allow time for the hot flash, and potentially embarrassing attention to it, to pass and enable her to return to business at hand, undistracted.

We must continue to break the silence and misconceptions around menopause by having more open and unapologetic conversations, not only with our health-care providers, but between genders and generations. This necessity to move toward more open communication falls on us all.

Welcome Midlife Beauty

My research data unequivocally reveals that physical appearance issues are a *relatively* low midlife concern. And yet we are bombarded with messages trying to convince us that wrinkles, muffin tops, and sagging skin are our pain points. Society celebrates youth and wants us to believe that youthful beauty is the only form of beauty. Entire industries try really hard to convince us to spend oodles of money on products and procedures so that we can look like we did in decades prior. But they do not really know us. Of course, we want to look and feel our best. But those products, while perhaps giving us a brief and superficial boost, do nothing for our deeper and more pressing concerns—our loved ones' passing, our children's well-being, and our financial stability, to name a few.

Beyond lovingly accepting our aging bodies, what can we do? We can challenge societal beauty standards by redefining aging as natural and beautiful. We can welcome our mature beauty rather than striving to look like we did in our thirties. We can appreciate the years of laughter behind our laugh lines. And, we can make choices based on our own desires, rather than societal pressure.

If you want to go gray, go gray. If you want to color your hair, then do it. If you want to get Botox, go for it. My goal is for us to ensure that we make these choices based on our individual desires, as opposed to in reaction to society's obsession with youthful beauty.

My friend Joni shared that she is enjoying the freedom of not coloring her hair, but she receives constant pushback from friends and family, who prefer her previously colored blonde hair. She is more distressed by their unsolicited feedback than the transitional phase of growing out her gray hair. Let's support and celebrate our friends' choices, regardless of what they are, and especially if they are different from ours.

Dara Goldberg, a woman I "met" on LinkedIn, is taking on the beauty industry's contribution to the anti-aging phenomena. She challenges companies whose messages equate youth with beauty, and invites women to join her bandwagon. Her mission is to encourage us to avoid supporting companies that promote these anti-aging beauty messages. There are also magazines which exclusively include women forty and older and others that will only use untouched photos. Subscribe to one of those even if you still enjoy your *Vogue*.

Most importantly, replace self-criticism with self-compassion. That is a deeper, longer lasting fix than any aesthetic procedure.

Looking for a role model? Jamie Lee Curtis is an amazing advocate for celebrating aging, including changes to our physical appearance. In a "Radically Reframing Aging Summit," hosted by Maria Shriver and the publishing company Sounds True, Jamie spoke of the need to reassess how we talk about aging. She emphasized that "This word 'anti-aging' has to be struck. I am pro-aging. I want to age with intelligence and grace and dignity and verve and energy," and "I don't want to hide from it (my age) as if it's a bad thing." Yes!

How we choose to approach our changing appearance is a personal decision. I still choose to color my hair, even as I am thrilled for and proud of my friends who are rocking their silver tops. Our collective mission is to embrace and showcase the beauty that is present at every age, to challenge the disempowering narrative that beauty is equated with a youthful appearance, and to support each other in our respective choices.

As midlife women, we have a depth of beauty that extends far beyond the mirror. While embracing the changes in our physical appearance, remember to recognize and celebrate the myriad forms of beauty that transcend our shells—the beauty of humor, kindness, sensitivity, and generosity. Embracing these qualities not only enhances our own sense of self-worth but also serves as a powerful reminder that beauty truly knows no physical bounds.

Advocate Against Stereotyping, Sexism, and Ageism

Stereotypes

Given my professional emphasis, research, and age, I now see negative stereotypes of midlife women everywhere: in advertising, in portrayals of women in movies, and as a topic for comedians' jabs.

Though there seems to be an increase in older female heroines, portrayals of middle-aged women in the media still skew negatively. We are more commonly represented along a continuum from boring to downright insulting. Our characters are often portrayed as frazzled, superficial, and insecure, and when they break free from their children, they gather at a bar to drink. We are too frequently still depicted as desperate to look younger in order to keep the interest of our silver-haired partners, lest we risk them being enticed away by younger women (as if we somehow should be held responsible for middle-aged men who may stray in reaction to their own midlife issues and insecurities).

Such media portrayals of middle-aged women are rude, wildly inaccurate, and perpetuate negative stereotypes and "crisis" myths. These recurring depictions can influence women to believe that a "crisis" is inevitable and, in worst-case scenarios, may even result in self-fulfilling prophecies. When there are relatively few examples of women in roles that challenge these stereotypes, it becomes harder to dismantle these myths and beliefs.

I remember how shocked I was the first time my husband and I saw a commercial for a local plumbing company. The scene was in a kitchen, where a couple lamented their clogged sink. When the male plumber arrives, he shakes hands with the slender and handsome husband without even acknowledging the wife's existence. The wife, dowdy and plump, silently stands smiling in the background. When the commercial ended, my husband and I looked at each other in stunned disbelief of this woman's negative portrayal. Though I knew we would never use that plumbing company, I wish I had thought to call the television station to submit a complaint.

What can we do? Boycott movies, shows, and products that diminish us in their advertising or content. Speak out against them, directly or via social media. Tell them how their portrayals of midlife women make us feel and why we will not buy their products. Unless we raise our voices and complain, and stop financially supporting them, how will they know to change?

Along with the condemnation of these negative stereotypes, we should use our networks and communities to promote and support movies, companies, and actresses who empower us, or at least authentically represent and depict our reality. Three of my favorite midlife actresses and roles are Michelle Yeoh in *Everything Everywhere All at Once,* Jean Smart in *Hacks,* and Hannah Waddingham in *Ted Lasso.* Their characters are smart, funny, and powerful. Another example is *Menopause the Musical.* This comedy musical revue is about four very different midlife women who bond over the shared challenges of aging and menopause. It is both educational and celebratory.

Sexism and Ageism

In December 2023, cultural essayist Shaan Sachdev contacted me and my colleague and friend Dr. Ken Druck to discuss an op-ed article he was writing for the *Wall Street Journal* about aging stars. The resulting article was titled "Beyoncé the Athlete is Adjusting to Midlife."[24] The writer explained that Beyoncé was criticized for dancing less vigorously on her Renaissance tour (a tour, according to Live Nation, in which she brought in more than $579 million), and he was curious if this kind of judgment of aging athletic women is common. I was angry at Beyoncé's critics (Seriously? Have you seen her moves on the movie of that tour?) yet not surprised by his question. "Yes," I said unequivocally, "and especially when you age in the public eye." I explained that physical decline is one of our top burdens, and that this is exacerbated for famous women by the perception that they should be able to look and do the same things in their forties and fifties as they could in their thirties. "Somehow we think Beyoncé has this superhuman capacity to defy aging," he quoted me in the article.

---

[24]   https://www.wsj.com/arts-culture/music/
beyonce-the-athlete-is-adjusting-to-midlife

For women, ageism (prejudice or discrimination based on a person's age) and sexism often intertwine in midlife. "Why is it that women with gray hair are perceived as no longer useful while men are described as seasoned?" posed one interviewee. Good question.

The American Association of Retired Persons (AARP) published a study in 2022 in which they polled 6,643 women about their experience of discrimination.[25] In their sample, almost sixty-six percent of the women aged fifty and older reported being subject to discrimination. Within this subset, ageism was the most frequent type, reported by forty-eight percent of the study subjects. For many, the experience of discrimination had he ripple effect of adversely impacting their mental and financial health.

Many of my interviewees, who work in corporate settings, shared their experiences of ageism relative to their competencies. Their colleagues repeatedly made erroneous assumptions relative to their skills, or rather perceived lack of skills. Kathleen worked in a traditionally male-dominated technology industry. "They assume that because I'm an older woman, I don't understand anything about technology. I've got twenty-plus years of hands-on experience and make it a point to stay up-to-date. I could be teaching them this shit!" she angrily exclaimed.

Lorna stated that she was involved in projects where she was intentionally "set up for failure" because she is a woman; "the decisions were literally impossible." Several women shared the experience of feeling penalized at work for placing their children's needs over their job.

Feeling less secure in their jobs in midlife was another common experience of the interviewees. Some were frustrated over hitting unjustified glass ceilings, while others questioned their longevity in

---

[25]   aarp.org/health/conditions-treatments/info-2022/
        women-discrinination-and-mental health.html

professions with patriarchal preferences or a desire for younger female employees. Brianna excels as a sales representative in the wellness industry, yet she repeatedly was passed over for promotions. Despite her experience and established record of success, the more visible jobs were frequently given to women in their twenties and thirties. Brianna said, "I know it's because they think a woman in her fifties no longer looks the part, but I'm scared to say anything or quit because I'm not sure I could get hired anywhere else in this industry."

Carla left her corporate career to serve on the school board of a huge school district, earning a pittance of her previous salary. It was a decision based on her passion to make education accessible to all, and she loves being in a position to influence that outcome. However, her tenure will end when she is sixty-two and, despite her stellar resume, she's fearful that she may not be hired elsewhere at that age. For Carla, the cost of taking the school board position, in spite of the financial setback and future security, was personally worth it. Thank you, Carla.

These stories reflect real discrimination in the workplace. And there is more evidence of discrimination. The majority of Chief Executive Officers (CEOs) in the 1,000 largest companies are in their fifties. Of these CEOs, a whopping ninety-four percent are male![26] Even more infuriating is a March 2024 article in *CEO Magazine* titled "In 2023, Women CEOs Finally Outnumbered CEOs Named John." The eye-opening (or perhaps jaw-dropping) title includes sobering statistics. "Only eight percent of CEO positions in the S&P 500 are held by women, and yet they represent more than fifty percent of the United States' population. In contrast, men named John represent only 3.27 percent of the United States' population, and until recently, had greater representation than women among S&P 500 CEOs."

---

[26]   https://chiefexecutive.net/ceo1000-key-trends-among-the-to
        p-1000-ceos/.

Both of these articles imply that while women are being subjected to ageism and sexism, males in middle age (especially those named John) are at the top of the corporate ladder.

Invisibility

In addition to experiencing discrimination, many women talked about being less noticed in midlife, sometimes to the degree of seeming invisible. They described feeling empty and irrelevant when their presence was barely acknowledged. This experience was a notable shift from their younger decades. Ali shared her experience of invisibility when she goes to the gym. She said, "It doesn't matter if I wash my hair or wear makeup. I'm invisible without my youth." Once, when she picked up her phone, the face recognition application would not give her access. Ali joked that even her phone does not "see" her anymore.

For several of the women I interviewed, the experience of invisibility was especially notable at the workplace. Their male colleagues, and even their younger female colleagues, increasingly undermined or ignored them; they talked over them or around them. In midlife, women are often at the peak of their competence and confidence—a powerful combination that should be embraced rather than ignored or rejected. Companies that subscribe to sexist and ageist practices are shooting us, and themselves, in the foot.

How to address discrimination

As with menopause, we can bring greater awareness to the reality of discrimination by talking about it. Imagine if even a moderate portion of those thousands of women discriminated against in the AARP survey shared their experiences. If you experience or witness ageism or sexism, get support and call it out together. We have greater safety and power in numbers. We can educate the discriminators that their comments are hurtful and unkind—and are not based in reality—drawing attention to their sexist and ageist biases. By speaking up, we are empowering ourselves to be visible in that moment. I am fully aware of how difficult this may be, but when we educate even one person, it makes a difference. If you are uncomfortable yet called to act, consider a report to human resources. At the very least, it could be the start of a paper trail.

Join and become a part of this important bandwagon. Say no to those companies whose messages and actions are sexist and/or ageist and thwart our deserved advancements. Nothing gets a company's attention faster than customer engagement and reduced revenues; be mindful whose bank accounts you want to support.

Lift Each Other Up!

I believe one of the most wonderful aspects of being a woman in midlife is that we have each other's back. Mostly gone is the competition and scarcity mentality of our younger decades. Not that competition is absent; many of us are competitive by nature, and we may work in environments that promote competition. But we increasingly appreciate that there is more than enough to go around and want to lift each other up in solidarity; we understand that a win for one of us is a win for all. I have experienced this support firsthand and seen its transformative power in my workshops and groups.

We can keep this momentum building by actively and openly supporting each other. Share the successes of women in your circle, and female celebrities, who have found new passions or defied age-limited goals. The story of extraordinary swimmer Diana Nyad, recently made into a movie (*Nyad*) starring Annette Bening and Jodi Foster, celebrates the defiance of age limitations. When she was sixty-four, after five attempts, Nyad succeeded in her lifelong goal of swimming from Cuba to Florida, 110 miles. Now that is a great story and movie to promote!

Celebrate women who are making significant contributions to their communities during this stage of life. Maria Shriver is one such person. She is an extraordinary advocate for women's rights, health needs, and a more positive narrative on aging. Her award-winning newspaper, the *Sunday Paper: For a Life Above the Noise*, includes a regular section that's titled "Radically Reframing Aging," with uplifting and informative content on aging.

By shining a spotlight on women's achievements, we not only celebrate their value but also inspire and empower other women in midlife to embrace their offerings. Make one such woman your role model. You can use her accomplishments as inspiration to fuel your own.

In the words of Alexandra Elle, a bestselling author, wellness educator, and podcaster, "Celebrating another woman's triumphs or success will never take away from your shine or glory. If anything, it'll add to and create more light."

The Bottom Line

This chapter could have been called "Embracing the Collective Middle," as all of the areas discussed above serve women collectively as well as individually. When we use our midlife wisdom and confidence to talk openly about menopause, challenge stereotypes and anti-aging messages, and advocate against sexism and ageism, change happens for us all. And we pave the way, an easier path, for future generations of women.

Conclusion

The middle decades are steeped in changes and transitions: menopause, deaths of loved ones, physical decline, caretaking demands, and empty nests are among the profound, lifechanging markers of this period. Because of these natural endings and consequent new beginnings, midlife is a perfect time to take stock of our lives—to examine, reflect, and ultimately reckon with what is calling for change. It is a time to question if we are living in alignment with our truest selves and to make any necessary shifts while there is still time. This process can be fueled by the changes happening both within and around us, and it can be deepened by our increased wisdom and self-awareness.

In midlife, we are flush with decades of life experiences and able to see ourselves and the world with more clarity. We have earned wisdom, and we have cultivated a wider emotional bandwidth that simply could not exist without the lessons and hardships of time. We are blessed to have reached midlife and with luck, will be blessed with many more decades ahead, to not only enjoy the gifts of age, but to use them to live our most authentic, rewarding life.

To embrace midlife is to be courageous. It is to walk through life as it is right now, with our eyes and hearts open, and to feel and experience the totality of it all. Though presence to lifechanging tides may not always feel good, it is real and ultimately liberating. Trying to ignore these changes and pushing away the discomfort is like putting a lid on a pot of boiling water. It will eventually blow the lid off, overflow, and make a mess. Instead, our earned wisdom can direct us on our midlife journey, and self-compassion can soften the ride. Indeed, there will be times when a glass of wine or a movie are exactly what we need. But when they are finished, presence and compassion can be our trusted companions as we continue on our journey.

Through our choices and our voices, we can shift the narrow, negative, and outdated narrative around midlife to a broader, more realistic, and more empowered one. I encourage us to embrace the entire tapestry and use our earned wisdom as our guide, not only for ourselves, but for our daughters, nieces, and granddaughters.

Whether or not you choose to "Embrace the Middle," I wish you grace, joy, fulfillment, and ease in the middle years and beyond. I close this book and bid you farewell with the words we chant at my local Zen Center:

"Time swiftly passes by and with it, our only chance. Each of us must aspire to awaken. Be aware. Appreciate this precious life."

With a deep bow to your presence, compassion, and wisdom.

APPENDICES

Appendix 1

SURVEY FACTORS

My survey data includes quantitative findings derived from survey questions numerically rated by the respondents. I supplemented the quantitative findings with qualitative data culled from interviews with a subset of women, wherein I asked open-ended questions.

When considering my data, it is important to note several factors:

1. 619 respondents are a relatively large sample size. This means that the quantitative results would likely not change if I added more respondents with a similar demographic makeup. The exception is the more detailed analyses regarding country of origin provided in Appendix 2. Those sample sizes are smaller. Future studies, with more respondents from different continents, could shed more light on any differences.

2. As mentioned in the Introduction, the survey was not intentionally designed to be a research study. It morphed into one when it organically spread to hundreds of women. I am thrilled by the number of participants. However, I unfortunately did not collect data on ethnicity or try to ensure diversity in other demographic areas, including marital status and work status.

   Of the 619 women who reported their marital and work status, the majority were married and working at least part time. Within the interviewee subsample of 103 women, which enabled me to directly inquire about ethnicity, it skewed toward Caucasian women. The implication of this is that the results may be more applicable to this subsample (i.e., white, married, working) of midlife women.

3. The answers to the survey questions were limited to pre-determined categories. That is, I decided which options to include, based on my personal and professional experience, under challenges and gifts. However, every question included an "other" category where women can and did add comments.

    This means that the survey results capture the most and least challenging and positive aspects of the pre-determined categories but obviously not of those excluded from the categories. In relaying my results, the one exception to sharing data beyond predetermined categories was the inclusion of "death and loss" as a top midlife challenge. My rationale is that it came up in virtually every single interview as a foremost concern and was also frequently cited in comments within the survey.

4. The survey was completed between March and December 2020, an interesting time for us all. This is the period when COVID began its advance throughout the world, when lockdowns and major restrictions were in place, and before vaccines were available. Even though the question was worded to have women consider their pre-pandemic life, it is likely that what was happening in the world at the time still impacted their answers. But, as every single respondent was dealing with the ramifications of COVID, it was a universal factor for all survey takers. Furthermore, as the virus continues to be a factor for the foreseeable future, there is less of a demarcation between a pre-COVID and post COVID existence.

Appendix 2

Additional Research Findings

As explained in Chapter 2, my data findings clustered together all women in their forties, fifties, and sixties. (Because there were far fewer women in their thirties and seventies who completed the survey, I excluded them from the analyses.) I relayed the collective results of respondents from those three decades within the manuscript.

Below, I share some interesting, statistically significant[27] findings regarding the gifts and challenges by age and country of residence. This study did not delve into why these differences exist. However, I will propose some possible explanations and relevant comments from interviewees. I also relay more findings relative to the specific challenge of hormonal fluctuations.

Age-Related Findings

1. "Hormonal changes/imbalances" were statistically significantly (i.e., subsequently referred to as significantly) more challenging for women in their forties and fifties, as compared to those in their sixties.

---

[27] Significance level $P<.05$

2. There was a significant increase in the experience of several of the "gifts" for women in their fifties and sixties, as compared to those in their forties. Specifically, "comfort in our skin," "less people-pleasing," "more me time," and "wisdom" were more "extremely resonant" for those in the older generations.

3. "Not sweating the small staff" was significantly more resonant for women in their sixties as compared to those in their forties.

4. Midlife presenting an "opportunity to re-evaluate my life and make changes" was significantly more resonant for women in their forties as compared to those in their sixties.

The bottom line of these preliminary findings is that the experience of midlife gifts significantly increases after our forties. Concurrently, our hormone-related challenges decrease after our fifties.

In 2018, Jonathan Rauch published *The Happiness Curve, Why Life Gets Better After 50.* Drawing on research, the author maintains that there is a U-shaped curve of happiness, with our forties representing the bottom of the curve of life satisfaction, before steadily climbing upward, beginning in the fifties. This unexpected phenomenon has been termed the paradox of aging. And, although his theory is based on data, it is not without criticism and dissent.[28]

If, and only if, we assumed (i.e., this was not directly asked on the survey) that the gifts described above resulted in a greater state of overall happiness or life satisfaction, my findings align with the Happiness Curve, when comparing the forties to the fifties and sixties, on those specific variables.

---

[28] Galambos, N. L., Krahn, H. J., Johnson, M. D., Lachman, M. E. (2020). "The U Shape of Happiness across the Life Course: Expanding the Discussion." *Perspectives on Psychological Science*, 15(4), 898– 912.

Menopause-Related Findings

One of the unexpected findings of the survey was the relatively lower ranking of changing hormones as a midlife concern. As discussed in Chapter 5, it is likely that some of the physical consequences of menopause are captured under the "physical/health" category of challenges as opposed to directly in the "hormonal changes" category of concerns. Indeed, there is a medium strong, positive, and significant correlation between hormonal changes and health/body decline. This at least statistically confirms that hormonal changes concerns are strongly related to health/body decline concerns. Consistent with these statistical findings, many of the specific physical challenges women discussed in the interview were difficulties that are often a function of menopause (e.g., impaired sleep, fatigue, etc.).

As discussed in chapter 11, many women are not educated by their health providers to appreciate that some of their physical challenges can actually be a result of menopause. Therefore, they may have not considered some of their health challenges to be a function of hormones. I am a perfect example. Because my mother had dementia, I panicked when I developed memory lapses and difficulty with focus during perimenopause. Not one doctor I spoke with explained that this could be a result of my hormonal chaos. I only learned this many years later through my own research. Indeed, as my hormone levels stabilized post-menopause, my thinking became clearer. Had I taken this survey in the midst of this struggle, I would not have connected my memory challenges as a hormonal issue.

Another factor impacting how women categorically capture their menopause-related physical difficulties (i.e., under health issues or hormone challenges) is that there are not always definitive sources of physical challenges. For example, sleep impairment could be a function of lower hormone levels, caretaking stress, or both. This was addressed in a 2022 article published by Harvard Health Publishing titled "Perimenopause: Rocky Road to Menopause:" "It can be difficult to distinguish the hormonally based symptoms of perimenopause from more general changes due to aging or common midlife events—such as children leaving home, changes in relationships or careers, or the death or illness of parents. Given the range of women's experience of perimenopause, it's unlikely that symptoms depend on hormonal fluctuations alone."[29]

To compound matters for women struggling with menopause, there is also a medium strong, positive, and significant correlation between the challenge of hormonal changes and physical appearance challenges—and those, as well as physical/health concerns, are all negatively and significantly correlated with being more "comfortable in one's skin."

This means that women struggling with hormone challenges are also more concerned with physical appearance issues and are less comfortable "in their skin." Hormonal challenges appear to be a challenge "that keeps on giving."

Cultural Variations

With regard to differences between women in different countries, I was able to compare the subsets of women living in North America with those living in the European Union, due to the relatively larger number of responses from these regions. These subsamples included 191 North American women, largely living in the United States, and ninety-six European women, from many different countries. It must be emphasized that these comparative sample sizes are much smaller than the overall 619. Furthermore, the opinions of the interviewees shared below are drawn from their individual lives and may not align

---

[29] https://www.health.harvard.edu/womens-health/
perimenopause-rocky-road-to-menopause

with the experiences and beliefs of a larger sample of respondents or the larger cultural norms and rules within and between European countries.

Bearing those caveats in mind, here are a few significant findings:

1. North American women had significantly more financial and "health and body decline" concerns than women living in Europe.

2. European women had significantly more "existential questions of value, worth, direction, life" than women living in North America.

3. The only difference relative to gifts was that women in North America "extremely resonate" significantly more with "fulfilling friendships" than those living in Europe. In line with this finding, North American women were significantly more likely to find "talking with friends" to be an extremely helpful tool in managing challenges, as compared with the European sample.

Some factors, which can contribute to differing levels of money and health concerns between the two continents, could be due to the varied health-care systems, the nature and extent of social support systems, and/or attitudes and policies toward aging.

One respondent, who lived on both continents, wrote the following in the comments: "Retirement has been way more demanding than the career years. Mostly because our country (i.e., the US) lacks the systemic support systems that the Europeans and Canadians have. Amazing that the lack of parental leave, quality day care, and eldercare STILL primarily affects women to make up the difference, even at sixty-nine! My biggest regret in life is returning from living in Europe to live in the US."

Another interviewee, who lives in the Netherlands, offered a different perspective. She shared her frustration in the inability to get medication (even ibuprofen) within their health-care system and the requirement to deliver her child at home, with the help of a midwife, because she was not deemed high enough risk to give birth in a hospital.

Sheila, a sixty-seven-year-old interviewee, who has lived in both the United States and Israel during her sixties, feels that younger generations in Israel have more respect for their elders than those in the States. Sheila feels more "valued" and is encouraged to share her wisdom living in Israel. She also stated that there is an implicit expectation in Israel that kids will care for their parents. When living in the United States, Sheila was "always exhausted and worried about money."

An interviewee who lives in Luxembourg stated that because health care is covered, she does not feel any financial stress over future medical needs. Furthermore, she has enjoyed getting several advanced degrees because education is free in Luxembourg.

Stella, who has lived in both the US and the UK during menopause, commented that "people in the UK are much more open to talking about menopause." She added that there are many more resources, support, and accommodations in the UK, even within corporations, for menopausal women. I would add that vaginal estrogen creams, which require a prescription in the United States, are available over the counter in several countries within the UK.

I am at a loss to explain the differential findings of more existential concerns and less fulfilling friendships for women in Europe as compared with those living in North America. Perhaps with fewer worries concerning money and health care, women in Europe have more bandwidth to explore existential issues. This is only speculation.

Exploring the cultural context of these two areas was not a regular interview topic.

Another comment relative to culture overall was the attitude toward therapy. A number of women shared the challenge of living in countries where therapy is still somewhat stigmatized. It impacts both their decision of whether to pursue therapy and their comfort in talking about it with others if they chose to get this type of help.

These results reflect some interesting preliminary differences between women living on these two continents, and between ages, but they are only preliminary. That being said, as is a theme of this book, the overall experience of midlife women appears to transcend cultural differences.

Appendix 3

INTERVIEWEES' BOOK RECOMMENDATIONS

A Course in Miracles, by Helen Schucman, 1976

A Different Truth: Reject the Truths That Are Killing Your Career, and Learn to Make Choices That Are Better for You, by Joanne Denton, 2018

A New Earth: Awakening to Your Life's Purpose, by Eckhart Tolle, 2005

Awareness: The Perils and Opportunities of Reality, by Anthony De Mello, 1990

Becoming, by Michelle Obama, 2018

Being Zen: Bringing Meditation to Life, by Ezra Bayda, 2003

Big Magic: Creative Living Beyond Fear, by Elizabeth Gilbert, 2016

Breaking the Habit of Being Yourself: How to Lose Your Mind and Create a New One, by Joe Dispenza, 2023

Bridging Two Realms: Learn to Communicate with Your Loved Ones on the Other Side, by John Holland, 2018

Come As You Are: The Surprising New Science That Will Transform Your Sex Life, by Emily Nagoski, 2015

Conversations with God: An Uncommon Dialogue, by Neale Donald Wasch, 1997

Dare to Lead: Brave Work. Tough Conversations. Whole Hearts., by Brené Brown, 2018

Do One Thing Different: Ten Simple Ways to Change Your Life, by Bill O'Hanlon, 2019 (rev.)

Everyday Zen: Love and Work, by Charlotte Joko Beck, 2007

Finding Your Own North Star: Claiming the Life You Were Meant to Live, by Martha Beck, 2002

Fly While You Still Have Wings: And Other Lessons My Resilient Mother Taught Me, by Joyce Rupp, 2015

Help, Thanks, Wow: The Three Essential Prayers, by Anne Lamott, 2012

Lean In: Women, Work, And the Will to Lead, by Sheryl Sandberg, 2013

Law of Attraction: The Science of Attracting More of What You Want and Less of What You Don't, by Michael J. Losier, 2011

Love Your Body: A Positive Affirmation Guide for Loving and Appreciating Your Body, by Louise Hay, 1998

Rising Strong: The Reckoning. The Rumble. The Revolution., by Brené Brown, 2015

The Artist's Way: A Spiritual Path to Higher Creativity, by Julia Cameron, 1992

The Art of Happiness, by 14th Dalai Lama and Howard C. Cutler, 2009

The Dance of Anger: A Woman's Guide to Changing the Patterns of Intimate Relationships, by Harriet Lerner, 2014 (paperback)

The Five Love Languages: The Secret to Love That Lasts, by Gary Chapman, 2024 (reprint)

The Four Agreements, by Don Miguel Ruiz, 2000

The Joy Plan: How I Took 30 Days to Stop Worrying, Quit Complaining, and Find Ridiculous Happiness, by Kaia Roman, 2017

The Power of Now: A Guide to Spiritual Enlightenment, by Eckhart Tolle, 1999

The Sleep Revolution: Transforming Your Life, One Night at a Time, by Arianna Huffington, 2016

12 Rules for Life: An Antidote to Chaos, by Jordan P. Peterson, 2018

The Secret, by Rhonda Byrne, 2007

The Shift: How I Lost (and Found) Myself After 40 – And You Can Too, by Sam Baker, 2021

The Untethered Soul: The Journey Beyond Yourself, by Michael A. Singer, 2007

The Wisdom of Love: Toward a Shared Inner Life, by Jacob Needleman, 2005

The Wisdom of the Enneagram: The Complete Guide to Psychological and Spiritual Growth for the Nine Personality Types, by Don Richard Riso and Russ Hudson, 1999

When Things Fall Apart: Heart Advice for Difficult Times, by Pema Chodron, 2016

Wisdom of Menopause: Creating Physical and Emotional Health During The Change, Christiane Northrup, 2006

Women, Food, and God: An Unexpected Path to Almost Everything, by Geneen Roth, 2011

You Are a Badass: How to Stop Doubting Your Greatness and Start Living an Awesome Life, by Jen Sincero, 2013

ACKNOWLEDGEMENTS

Writing *Embrace the Middle* was a three-year journey—a journey which included the deaths of my father and brother and many other midlife changes and challenges. Though I did not appreciate it at the time, navigating these profoundly difficult chapters was my real-life graduate training to write this book; I was tasked with walking my talk. There were many months when I was overcome with sorrow and had to stay present to my grief rather than write, and many other months when self-doubt and life got in the way of writing. But I persevered.

Throughout the entire time, my amazing husband Eric was my rock. His love, support, encouragement, shared brainstorming, and editing of my writing was endless. I am so grateful to be married to him. I love you, Eric, and the life we have created.

My daughters Tara and Maya taught me about the power and beauty of sisterhood, something I did not experience growing up in a household with four brothers. They are incredible in their own right, inspire me, and have shared in my excitement in every stage of this book. I absolutely love being their mom.

I am very fortunate to have had some wonderful Zen teachers over the decades: Ezra Bayda, Elizabeth Hamilton, Diane Moore, Rabbi Lavey Darby, and others who taught me from a distance. Their teachings live within me and are paramount to embracing. I am deeply grateful to each of you and for the many hours and retreats we sat together over the years.

I am profoundly indebted to each of the 619 women who completed the survey and the 103 who volunteered to be interviewed. Your generosity of time, information, wisdom, and stories are an integral part of this book and a gift of validation and support to all women. Thank you.

Along the way, there were a number of women who kept me on track. Sarah McArthur helped get me started and Amberly Finarelli, of Authority Publishing, guided me across the finish line. In the middle, my beta readers Kate Byrne, Julie Gothard, Michele Hebert, Jo Pastore, Evelyn Wells, and Diane Zeigler offered valuable input. Special shoutout to my friend, dharma sister, and beta reader Virgina Reuter for editing multiple iterations and to Kelley Kurtzman, for your support of every phase of the journey. I am deeply grateful to each of you.

Belia Schuurman, a statistics teacher at Leiden University, generously offered statistical input and guidance. Thank you, Belia!

Lastly, my village of friends and family is wide and deep. Many of you helped spread the survey, were interviewed, had a front row seat to this book's evolution, and offered encouragement and support along the way. Thank you. I am so very blessed to have you all in my life.

With Deep Appreciation,
Shayna

About the Author

Dr. Shayna Kaufmann is a clinical psychologist, certified mindfulness meditation teacher, decades-long Zen practitioner, and founder of Embrace the Middle—a company dedicated to serving women in midlife. Her teachings, workshops, and meditation gatherings guide women to bring more authenticity, presence, and self-compassion into their lives. Shayna is a published researcher, a community volunteer, popular speaker, and former faculty at Alliant International University and National University. She lives in San Diego with her husband, Eric, and dog, Nola, named after her hometown of New Orleans, and treasures visits from their daughters, Tara and Maya.

 EmbraceTheMiddle.com
 @ShaynaKaufmann
 Shayna Gothard Kaufmann
Embrace The Middle

SOFTT

S - Slow down and breathe

O - Observe your thoughts & emotions

F - Feel into your bodily sensations

T - Tenderly place hand to heart, "this is hard."

T - Tune-In to your inner wisdom

EmbraceTheMiddle.com

Keep SOFTT handy for reference.
Take a picture or cut this out and use it as a bookmark.